LIES FROM GRANDMA'S GRAVE

By

Julie Mills & Jodie Meyer

Table of Contents

Dedication

This book is dedicated to all of mom's children, grandchildren and great grandchildren. May you find comfort in these pages in having just a piece of her near to your heart. Although some of you may not have known her in the flesh, she loved BIG, and openly, and she would have loved us all.

We also want to dedicate this book to Jamie Lee Hasse and Jakwan Shakur Shepherd, two of mom's grandchildren who are now resting in heavenly peace. Thank you for guiding us you two beautiful angels! All three of you gone, but NEVER forgotten. Until we meet again. We love you to the moon and back!

Acknowledgments

In loving memory of our Mother Beverly, whose life story graces these pages, and to every reader who finds a piece of themselves in these pages, may you find the strength and courage to tell your truth.

About the Authors

Julie

Julie never imagined she would become an author, but life has a way of unfolding in unexpected ways. A proud mother of eight and soon-to-be grandmother of eight, she spent twenty-one years in the utility industry before returning to college later in life to complete her degree in Business Management, which was a long-held dream finally realized.

Writing this book with her sister, Jodie, became much more than a project. It was a calling and a way to honor their mother, Beverly, whose story of strength, suffering, and resilience had long been buried under lies and silence. For Julie, this journey has been both healing and humbling, allowing her to understand her family's history through new eyes and to give voice to a woman who had been denied her own.

When she isn't studying or writing, Julie finds joy in simple pleasures: reading a good book, watching horror movies, dancing with family and friends, and planning her next adventure. She adores the fall season, finds comfort in all things *Winnie the Pooh*, and cherishes every moment spent surrounded by the people she loves most.

Jodie

Jodie has devoted her life to caring for others, first as a daycare provider for 34 years, then in retail, and now as a retiree who finds joy in crocheting and sharing her handmade creations at craft shows. She and her husband, Tom, have been married for 49 years and are the proud parents of three children.

This memoir, co-written with her youngest sister, Julie, is Jodie's first published work. It was born out of an emotional reunion that reunited the sisters after decades apart — a reunion that revealed the truth about their mother, Beverly, and the lies that had long divided their family. Through honesty, compassion, and courage, Jodie brings her voice and heart to this book, sharing a story of survival, resilience, and reconnection.

She hopes that others who have endured manipulation, family trauma, or separation will find comfort, strength, and solidarity within these pages.

Jodie also wishes to express her heartfelt gratitude to three extraordinary women named **Cindy R., Mary Lou, and Sandy C.**, who entered her life at different times and offered the simple yet profound gift of listening. Their love and encouragement helped her find the courage to share her truth with the world.

"Speak the truth, even if your voice shakes." — Unknown

Prologue

In the shadows of our family's history lies a tale of unspeakable cruelty and profound resilience. This book serves as a beacon to illuminate the harrowing journey of our mother, a woman whose life was ensnared in the web of manipulation, abuse, and heartache spun by her own mother.

For too long, our mother has been cast as the villain in a narrative woven from a tapestry of deceit and betrayal. Behind closed doors, she endured relentless mental and physical abuse at the hands of her own flesh and blood, inflicted by the very woman who should have offered solace and protection.

But the depths of our mother's suffering extend beyond the confines of her own pain. She endured the unbearable agony of having her precious children torn from her embrace, their innocence tainted by the venomous lies woven by the one who should have nurtured them with love.

For decades, our mother bore the weight of this burden alone, her spirit fractured but never broken. Yet, after a lifetime of separation and sorrow, fate intervened, and the long-lost bonds of siblinghood were rekindled after sixty-five years of silence.

In the wake of this reunion, the veil of deception was lifted, revealing the truth that had long been shrouded in darkness. Our mother's children, once estranged and alienated, discovered the heartbreaking reality of the lies that had poisoned their perception of her.

This book is more than just a memoir—it is a testament to the resilience of the human spirit and the enduring power of love in the face of unspeakable adversity. It serves as a clarion call to all who bear witness, urging them to recognize the signs of abuse and to extend a hand of compassion and support to those in need.

May our mother's story serve as a guiding light, illuminating the path towards healing, redemption, and the triumph of the human spirit over darkness.

Chapter 1: Born into despair

Strange how we, humans, are born crying into this world. There's no memory of that, but we all know that leaving the warmth of the womb and being delivered into a colder environment is what marks the beginning of our unique journey into this world.

The mother's warmth assuages the hysterical cries, and we, as babies feel the familiarity and recognize the warmness that was so lovingly carried with for months. In the recesses of remembrance, this distressing yet impactful initial phase of our lives plots a tale of a time when motherly love became a longing, a search for unknown solace.

But what if that warmth never comes?

At each phase of life, we are reborn into different personalities, into a different world, into a different character. Likewise, Beverly Miller's remains cold and loveless. A world brimming with potential and possibility welcomed Beverly Miller, soon to be turned into a heart ensnarled by the realities of maternal indifference.

There were memories of merriment, of crying and consoled by someone mother-like, of snuggling with someone mother-like... Then there's a void filled with the palpable absence of all that. It was as if it was never there... like Beverly Miller's mother was never there.

She is not your mother... all that remains were the constant echoes like a bitter elixir forced to be gulped down. There was home, there was someone mother-like, there was a family... then there were the permanent residents in the name of longing and abandonment.

Gloom replaced glee, silent rebuff replaced snuggles, and cries and complaints became inconsolable and then soundless. The unmistakable but unacceptable desertion seeped into the heart and mind gradually, thoroughly, and insidiously. The terms of endearment were a foreign language, the words of appreciation a far-fetched idea, and the feeling of a family remained a stranger to Beverly Miller's household.

***

It wasn't the days of peace and tranquility as the world was teetering on the brim of the next global catastrophe — so were Genevieve L. Marshall and Everett J. Martin. Dressed in a rayon fabric gown and sporting a hat embellished with a brooch and net veil, Genevieve sighed, fixing the tilt of her hat. The long gloves matched the purse and shoes, while her soft smile remained the eye-catcher.

Exiting the room designated for brides, Genevieve strutted down the hallway with one of her bridesmaids following behind. The hallway was rather deserted, given that it was the days when most couples were getting married regardless of the persisting impact of the Great Depression. The peering flickers of sunlight evinced that it was almost time to get to the altar. The mallet-like thud grew louder and faster as Genevieve quickened her pace to get to the altar. As she reached the threshold of the church, the bridesmaid grabbed her shoulder and handed her an elaborate bouquet of roses, lilies, and carnations.

Dressed in a patterned coat with shoulder pads and a striped tie with a felt hat, Everett fashioned a thin mustache in an attempt to appear en vogue for his wedding with Genevieve. The church featured crystal chandeliers and a few occupied rows of pews. The invitees turned around, eyeing the bride in white. Genevieve walked towards the altar, constantly fixing the tilt of her hat and placing the netted veil. Everett extended a hand as she reached the altar, now smiling from ear to ear. The bridesmaids, dressed in pastel colors, lined up behind the bride while the groomsmen, dressed in all black, took their positions behind Everett.

"In the name of the Father, and of the Son, and of the Holy Spirit," the priest began the ceremonial speech for the celebration of matrimony.

"Amen," the invitees said in unison.

"Grace to you and peace from God our Father and the Lord Jesus Christ," the priest continues.

"And with your spirit," the invitees responded.

"Dearly beloved, you have come together into the house of the church so that in the presence of the church's minister and the community, your intention to enter into marriage may be strengthened by the Lord with a sacred seal," the priest added.

"Everett and Genevieve, have you come here to enter into marriage without coercion, freely and wholeheartedly?" the priest inquired.

"I do," the couple responded.

The priest sprinkled the rings with holy water before the exchange of rings. With a twinkle in her eyes, Genevieve placed the ring on Everett's finger, and the two were pronounced husband and wife.

"In the sight of God and these witnesses, I now pronounce you husband and wife! You may now kiss!" the priest declared, and the invitees cheered as the bride and groom kissed.

The wedding ended with a reception dinner at the bride's home, including finger food, fruit punch, and an elegantly crafted, multi-tiered homemade wedding cake. March 11, 1939, marked the beginning of Mr. and Mrs. Everett J. Martin's ephemeral married life.

There was clamoring followed by loud name-screaming climaxing at inconsolable sobbing — which usually proved to be an event-turner — and ending with bed squeaking. As clichéd as it might sound, the marriage was in shambles, held together with self-guilt of the two sharing a room and bed.

The colonial-style Martin family house exhibited the ruins of Everett's and Genevieve's marriage, with the kitchen sink brimming with days-old filth, the torn-off cushions covering the front hall furnishings, and the constant mess that became an everyday sight and a Martin house norm. Genevieve was mostly found sleeping in her room or resting on the lounge sofa.

Everett lived with his widowed mother, four siblings, and a brother-in-law … the Great Depression had most families living together in a single house to reduce and manage the costs and household budget. The in-laws rarely ever saw their daughter-in-law out of her room; her tiredness seemed incessant. The Depression had a significant effect on employment; those who used to work in offices were now forced to opt for menial jobs, and Everett was one such fellow. Everett and his brother-in-law were the only two working to support the home. Everett worked as a laborer in a Park Maintenance project, and his brother-in-law was a milkman. He worked long, physically draining hours to provide for the home. The long shifts left him with no capacity to debate or reason.

The daily squabbles tainted all hopes to repair the damage done to their connubial relationship. The nuptial misery peaked on mention of divorcing each other upon the slightest argument — the in-laws perceive it as their self-manifestation.

Four months and a week later, on July 18, 1939, Genevieve filed for divorce. She accused her husband of failure to provide the necessities of life. She charged him with the inability to provide her with a separate home, food, and day-to-day clothing. The spacious courtroom with high ceilings and large windows allowed the natural light to spill in, casting long shadows on the polished wooden floors. The walls were paneled with dark wood, adding to the somber atmosphere. At the front of the room, the judge's bench was elevated, with a large American flag and the state flag behind it. The quietude of the room was punctuated with hushed whispers of the few spectators present.

Genevieve entered the courtroom with her lawyer, and the footfall of her block heel had Everett turn around. It was a reverberating reminder of the day the two became one. The screeching of the clerk's chair interrupted Everett's musing as he watched Genevieve smile and nod at her lawyer's propositions.

That was the last time Everett ever saw Genevieve smiling or, for that matter, her at all. Genevieve requested an alimony of $50 per month. In Everett's defense, Genevieve was never loyal to him and was involved with other men. The hearings and proceedings experienced delays due to the well-expected and ill-timed beginning of WWII. The courts remained closed for an extended and unknown period.

Two years and sixteen days later, on December 16, 1941, Everett and Genevieve were granted a divorce without any alimony granted to Genevieve. Throughout the legal proceedings, Genevieve only demanded alimony but received child support in the amount of $10 a month for Beverly Ann Martin, who was born on April 2,

1940. It's uncertain whether Everett ever knew or saw Beverly Ann Martin, leaving a lingering mystery for the little one.

Beverly Martin's birth turned out to be fortunate for Genevieve,

not because she gave birth to a beautiful baby, but because she would receive a good amount for this baby every month. Beverly was nothing more than a financial subsidy to Genevieve. The first look at her baby overwhelmed her, and a flood of emotions overwhelmed her. In that tiny face and fragile existence, Genevieve saw her unfulfilled dreams.

What if this child never let me be me? Genevieve's reluctance to accept the baby grew. *What if this girl never allowed me to live my life?* Genevieve heaved deeply. *What if my life becomes all about her? What about me then?* Her eyes glimmered with potential hope. *What if I leave this liability to my parents? they will surely take care of her for me,* Genevieve felt an intoxicating sense of relief and satisfaction. *Why not!? My parents can take care of her, and I can take care of my matter. Hallelujah!* A powerful desire to have more, be more kept Genevieve perpetually striving, chasing the wealth and thrill. For her, what she can acquire became the purpose of existence, though elusive, but forever satisfying. ….

"I won't be able to take care of her," Genevieve excused, handing her baby girl to her parents. To Genevieve's satisfaction and relief, Beverly Ann Martin was sent with her maternal grandparents, Lloyd and Edna Marshall, once the attending physicians released Genevieve and Beverly. Lloyd and Edna had this strange feeling that their daughter was telling the truth, or was it just her way of diverting from the responsibility?

"Why would she leave her child to us?" Edna wondered, questioning Genevieve's intent and plans. Edna rocked baby Beverly on the ride back home from the maternity clinic. The rhythmatic fall and rise of Beverly's tiny chest, the fluttering of her eyelids as the automobile jolted on road bumps, her suckling on the milk bottle – Beverly became the definition of Edna and Lloyd's lives of as grandparents.

"Would you hurry? I need to put her down. My arms hurts from carrying her all the way," Edna hastened her way to the bedroom and carefully put Beverly down on her bed. Lloyd stood towering over the tiny girl with an ear-to-ear smile.

"Ain't she a beauty?" Lloyd pecked Beverly's forehead.

Lloyd and Edna lived in Denton, Nebraska, in a small house with a yard and no children, as theirs were all adults now, or relatives. The simple gabled roof and symmetrical double-hung windows gave the house a quaint, inviting appearance. A small front porch, just big enough for a pair of rocking chairs, served as the entrance. The wooden door, painted a cheery shade of red, creaked slightly as it opened into the living room adjacent to the bedrooms. The master bedroom had a simple wooden bed frame with a hand-stitched quilt. The other two rooms were sparsely furnished, one with bunk beds for the children and the other serving as a guest room.

"You stay there, I will arrange the room for her," Edna announced as she unlocked the lock of bedroom with the bunk beds. Coughing, she took a broom and quickly removed the webs hanging in the far corner of the bedroom, ensuring nothing harms her beloved.

The late afternoon sun cast a golden glow through the lace curtains of the small, cozy bedroom. Humming an old tune, she smoothed the handmade quilt on the twin bed. The quilt, a patchwork of colorful squares, had been stitched with love and care over the years, each piece telling a story of its own. She fluffed the pillows, replaced the pillow covers with freshly ironed ones, and placed the pillows neatly at the head of the bed.

"Is she sleeping quietly?" Grandma Edna peeked out of the room to whisper-scream her queries. Lloyd gave her a thumbs up from their room as Edna hastened her cleaning chores. She carefully arranged a porcelain doll with a frilly dress, a small vase of wildflowers picked from the garden that morning, and a silver-framed photograph of her, Lloyd, and Genevieve with chubby faces beaming a toothless smile. Once sure of the arrangements of the room, she carefully, with silent footsteps, carried the little baby girl to her room.

Soon, the days of infancy became a thing of the past, and the cackles, blubberings, and playtimes of toddling Beverly echoed throughout Lloyd and Edna's modest home. Their day started with preparing Beverly's favorite breakfast, followed by stomach-hurting laughter, and ended with a new princess story each night for the grandparents' only princess.

Most evenings were spent playing and running around the backyard with Grandpa Lloyd in a blindfold.

"Where is my little sprinter? Is this you?" Flailing his arm in search of his princess, Grandpa Lloyd stumbled over a small rock, making Beverly shriek.

"You good, Pa?" the tiny voice was laden with worry.

"Got you! Now, I am all okay!" Grandpa Lloyd chuckled and tickled the belly of his little sprinter.

Wafting from the tiny kitchen window opening outside came the fresh, tempting aroma of apple pie – one of Beverly's favorite evening snacks. Inside, the scent of baked apple pie mingled with the earthy fragrance of the garden herbs drying by the window. Seated at the wooden table, the little sprinter swung her legs, her feet barely touching the worn floorboards.

"Ma, can I have apple pie all day on my birthday?" Beverly said, her eyes bright with excitement for the upcoming birthday.

Grandma Edna looked up from her properly divided apple pie, her weathered hands moving with practiced ease. Her eyes crinkled with a warm smile, the deep lines of her face a testament to decades of laughter and hardship. "Well, your birthday is quite far, princess."

Sitting next to Beverly and fixing a napkin around her neck, Grandpa Lloyd interjected, "If apple pie is what you want, an apple pie party is what you will have this birthday. Happy, sprinter?"

Beverly threw herself around Grandpa Lloyd's neck, "You know, I can't say no to my princess," he patted her frail shoulder.

"Best birthday ever!" Beverly guffawed, confident her sixth birthday would be the one to remember. The grandparents celebrated the apple-pie-themed birthday with full fervor, featuring home-cooked recipes and baked apple pie cake. Little Beverly had an ear-to-ear smile plastered on her face all day, with recurrent hugs and pecks to her grandparents.

The birthday became the talk of the town, and her biological mother got to hear about it, too. Just like Beverly, Lloyd, and Edna never declined any of Genevieve's wishes and requests, this time, Genevieve desired the most-loved thing Edna and Lloyd had.

"Mother, she is my daughter. And I can now take care of her myself," Genevieve presented assurance of Beverly's care.

"But, we are able to take care of her. We don't need anyone else. I don't think she will be comfortable going with you. After all, she has known only us as family. All these years…" Edna was rudely interrupted.

"What happened, happened. Now, I am taking responsibility for her. You can't tell me not to take my own daughter with me. This is enormous injustice," Genevieve put up a pretense of being teary-eyed. She took out a handkerchief from her purse and gently tapped her eyes.

"Look, Genevieve, what your mother is trying to say is that Beverly was never a burden for us; in fact, she makes us feel alive. And where have you been? Who do you live with?" Lloyd inquired, brows furrowed.

"Father, I am, once again, a married woman. I married Christian Miller – the owner of Miller Motels in Nebraska. And…" Genevieve pursed her lips and heaved.

"What now? Are you planning to leave him, too?" Lloyd inched forward from the backrest of their lounge sofa.

"And Christian and I have a baby boy named Teddy. He turned a year old in October." Genevieve wiped her philtrum, avoiding any eye contact with her parents.

"If that makes you happy, we don't have to say anything then," Lloyd cleared his throat and inquired in hushed tones, "Is Everett still sending you child support now that you have a child with another man?"

"Why would I refuse the extra $10? Yes, Beverly is still his child, and he is bound to take care of her," Genevieve spoke with a hint of indignation as she crossed her legs.

Beverly listened intently, peeking from the slightly ajar door of her room. Grandpa Lloyd's strict tone had her hugging her babydoll tightly. She knew she lived with her grandparents, but for her, they were all she ever had.

"I don't want to go…" Beverly mumbled, snuffling a little, "Ma, Pa, me… I don't want to go…"

The clinking of cutlery, discernible sighs, and perceptible sniffling silenced the arguments. Edna almost immediately looked over her shoulder upon hearing a muffled thud from inside.

"What if Beverly wants to go, too…" Edna placed a hand on Lloyd's shoulder, speaking under her breath. Lloyd held her other hand tightly, cleared his throat, and moved to be seated on the very edge of the sofa.

"Genevieve, we just moved to Arizona in our new home. We haven't even settled here yet. This place is new to Beverly and us, so let's not make it more difficult for that child.

But please don't take her away from us. And now… after all these years… what is the meaning of this?" Lloyd sipped his tea, placing the teacup on the lounge table.

"Well, I am not going anywhere from Nebraska, so you can come here to meet your granddaughter whenever you want," Genevieve quickly got up, hollering at her daughter, "Beverly, come on out. We will leave in a little while."

"Genevieve, listen… Genevieve…" Edna followed Genevieve to Beverly's room, where she found Genevieve kneeling and hugging already-weeping Beverly.

"My child, we have to leave. Momma's back. And I missed you so much…" Genevieve kissed her face, "I am never letting you out of sight again, my sweet baby."

13

"Will you excuse us for a moment, Genevieve?" Lloyd spoke firmly.

Lloyd gathered Beverly in his arms and had her seated on her bed beside Edna. "Look, sprinter, I know you are very little to understand all this, but you knew all along that we are your grandparents, not your actual parents, right?" Beverly nodded. "She is your real mother, and she has come to take you with her. She loves you more than we can, but we will always love you," Beverly's chin quivered. "She will take very good care of you. You will have all the toys in the world. And you will have a baby brother to play with. Isn't that exciting?" Beverly let the tears wet her face again.

Wiping Beverly's face with her sleeves, Edna sniffled, "You will have the best of apple pies there, too, even better than grandma's."

"You will forever be my sprinter and grandma's princess. If you don't like it, say it to momma, and we will take you with us, okay?" Lloyd hugged his granddaughter for the last time, letting her cry over his shoulder.

The suitcases were stacked and tied with a rope on the roof of the automobile Genevieve arrived in. She waved farewell to her parents, held Beverly's hands, and pushed her inside the automobile.

Edna and Lloyd remained outside their house, watching the automobile turn around the corner. The front yard looked like a sprawling meadow, with overgrown and untamed grass, sprouting fruits, and budding flora — marking a new beginning for Edna, Lloyd, and Beverly.

Ma, Pa, I will forever love you… home is you, and you are my home, Beverly Ann Martin was now the step-daughter of Christian Miller and Genevieve L Marshall.

Chapter 2: Betrayal in Disguise

"You want some cookies? Mom made it." Genevieve bit into a chocolate chip cookie, munching audibly.

Little Beverly forced a feeble smile and nodded in refusal.

"Have you ever traveled in trains, Beverly?" Genevieve tapped her finger on a black compact box and patted her lips, admiring herself in the small mirror.

"Noo…" Beverly answered in a weak voice.

"Oh, how exciting; you are going to have your first-ever train ride," Genevieve gestured to the driver to speed up.

The sky looks happy, turning all blue and bright, and Beverly leaned against the window, her nose almost touching the glass. The train whistled, followed by a chuffing sound, and Beverly was off to her new home.

Fields with cows, tiny as ants, spread out on either side, and every now and then, a windmill stood tall and strong with its spinning arms. Pinned to the glass window and agape, Beverly gazed at the world forming her vision.

It's the softest, bluest ever, Beverly pointed to the marshmallow-like big clouds. *Giant, yellow grass!* Beverly exclaimed at the fields the train passed by. *Ant-goats! Ant-goats!* Beverly gestured to Genevieve to look outside with her. Genevieve peeled and handed her a banana to munch on while she busied herself with fixing her hair. The wide grin died down into pressed-together lips. For the remaining train ride, Beverly watched with silent excitement the wonders of a journey.

"Beverly, get up!" Genevieve jolted her daughter up from sleep. "Grab this, and let's get going!" handing Beverly her backpack.

Off the train, the train station bustled with activity, with porters carrying luggage and passengers hollering for their families. The quick-service cafes had queues in front of them as people shouted their orders. The ticket counters situated in the corners were flooded with people inquiring and complaining. Public address systems made different announcements for arrivals, departures, and delays, adding to the raucousness. The grand large façade and spacious interiors seemed suffocating with people in such amounts — *silence seemed a stranger to this place.* People boarding the trains pushed through those arriving at the station, which made hollering a lot more relevant and understandable.

"Stay by my side, Beverly," Genevieve instructed in a strict tone.

Beverly clung to the hem of Genevieve's dress, stepping on to gooey stuff, "Mom, my shoe stick."

"Watch where you step, little girl!" Genevieve took off the shoe from Beverly's foot, "My car must be right outside. Walk barefooted for a while," Genevieve mumbled, "Now, I will have to buy her new shoes. Ughh."

The pavement felt boring hot beneath as Genevieve's grip tightened around her wrist. Her feet sprinting at a pace unknown. Beverly's complaints were lost amidst the clamor of people, the screeching of car brakes, and the distant wail of a train whistle. Beverly braved the situation, but that one naked foot hurt while the strap of her small backpack kept slipping off her shoulder. She could barely see where they were going, weaving through a sea of legs, dodging the suitcases and carry bags.

"Driver, bring the car out front!" Genevieve waved her handkerchief to signal the driver while Beverly tried regaining her composure and fighting the daze.

The automobile halted with a sudden jolt, stirring Genevieve up from her shuteye. After a series of reprimands and intimidations from Genevieve, the driver escorted the mother and daughter to the house's entrance. The imposing structure stood tall and wide with a wrap-around porch adorned with white columns. The house evinced Victorian elegance and modern 1940s comforts. Its large windows sparkled in the sunlight, and the intricate woodwork on the gables and eaves showcased the luxuries money could buy and offer.

A middle-aged maid welcomed the mother and daughter inside, pecking Beverly's forehead. Genevieve snapped her fingers, and the driver was quick to remove their luggage from the threshold and take it inside. Genevieve relaxed on the couch in the living room while Beverly stood silently with the maid, one foot shoeless still.

"Where is Teddy?" Genevieve asked no one in particular.

The maid, holding one hand of Beverly, guided her into the living room and had her seated on the couch adjacent to Genevieve's. A moment later, the maid came with a toddler chewing on a plastic car toy.

"Beverly, this is Teddy, your baby brother. Teddy, say hi," Genevieve said, grabbing her son in her arms. She removed his hand from the toy car and made him wave at Beverly.

Beverly smiled at her baby brother and got up to kiss him, but was abruptly stopped by her mother, "Wash your hands and face first. You can't touch him with filthy hands."

17

With one flick of Genevieve's hand, Beverly was removed from the living room and led to her room. The room appeared more of a makeshift storage space than a bedroom. The old paint was peeling from the ceiling and near the windows, with weathered wooden beams and cabinets on the top corners. The space smelled of cleaning chemicals with an occasional waft of stink exuding from a wet and unwashed mop leaning behind the door. The compact space was dimly lit by a singular, flickering bulb. The only decoration was a picture frame of mountains hanging from a rusty nail on one of the walls. The flickering bulb created an atmosphere of loneliness amidst the vast emptiness. The thin mattress on the iron-sculpted framework made up her bed, placed in the center.

"This is your room. You will stay here," the maid placed Beverly's suitcases on her bed, making the entire framework creak.

"Is she settled in her room?" Genevieve voiced her queries as the maid closed the door before leaving Beverly's new room. Beverly sat crossed-leg on her new bed, took out the babydoll from her backpack, and hugged it tightly – the babydoll was the first-ever gift Grandpa Lloyd gave her.

"Ma, Pa, I am scare," Beverly cried herself to sleep, missing her first family dinner with Mom, new Dad, and baby brother Teddy.

...few years later

The school bus screeched around the corner, dropping Beverly at the end of the street. The almost 11-year-old Beverly trudged down the street, carrying her and her baby brother's bag.

"How come Momma didn't come to pick you up today?" Beverly quizzed the now five-year-old Teddy. The little boy shrugged and walked with a waddle.

"There you are, my baby. Momma's sorry you have to come on the bus… so sorry. Tomorrow, we will have lunch at your favorite place, okay?" Genevieve took Teddy's bag from Beverly and gathered him in her arms.

"Momma, can I come, too? Tomor…" Beverly's enthusiasm to have lunch with her brother and mother was met with a grimace of disapproval.

"Who's momma good boy?" Genevieve tickled her baby boy, *making Teddy guffaw. "Momma, you're the best!" Teddy shed the happy tears, knowing his mother will always love him…* Beverly walked passed the sitting area, where Teddy and Genevieve would spend most of their afternoons and evenings. Their love-filled expression and giggles became incidental music for Beverly as she completed her daily after-school chores.

One last touch to smooth the bedsheet, Beverly smiled as her baby brother's giggles intensified. *Have to scrub this stain off the dish.* Genevieve's words of affection made her sigh as she tidily placed the dishes in the dish drying rack. *"Ow, ow, ow, something got in my eye!"* Teddy shouted, crashing his toy cars together with wild enthusiasm. The chaos brought a spark of life to Genevieve — something Beverly hadn't experienced and never would.

Most nights, Teddy would have Beverly read him stories, given her excellent narrating skills. Soon enough, unwillingly, Beverly developed an affection for her little brother. After all, who can hate a kid his age? Storytimes at night were the only instances in the Miller household when somebody would show any interest in talking to Beverly. The days passed with Beverly dutifully following the routine and doing the assigned chores.

"Hush, hush, you go to sleep… hush, hush, moon is here… hush, hush, baby Teddy is sleepy…" Beverly would sing her made-up lullabies to Teddy before leaving for her room.

Once alone in her bedroom in the darkness, the ten-year-old would plan out her entire day depending on the errands to manage time for both household and studies. However, most nights, the strained mind and body would simply give in to the overpowering slumber, shutting only the lethargic eyes.

The morning alarm peeled Beverly away from the much-needed rest. The alarm clock showed half-past five — she was an entire half-hour late. Fortunately, she spotted the garbage collecting truck at the very end of the street. Bare-footed and with two garbage bags in each hand, she ran towards the truck, screaming at the garbage man to wait for her. She shuffled from leg to leg, realizing her feet were hurt from the debris on the road.

As per the defined routine, she quickly brushed her teeth and washed her face, skipping the get-ready-for-school part. She cleaned her bedroom and hand-washed her dirty clothing as Momma trained her to do. Following that, she was supposed to water the plants in the backyard and dust the sitting area and living room. A minute away from missing her school bus, Beverly heaved a sigh on finding a seat on the school bus. She waved at her only friend in the neighborhood and, before long, was napping and snoring loudly.

"School's here," somebody jolted her back to reality.

Beverly's school was in Fairmont, which was a significant distance away from Miller's house. This allowed her to catch a nap on the bus rides to and from school.

As she approached the school, the sight of so many children swarming the playground, their laughter and chatter formed the school atmosphere. The bell tower stood tall, ringing the start of a new school day. Beverly pulled up the strap of her school bag, feeling both excitement and nervousness bubble within her. After the war, the American education system faced a severe teacher shortage caused by increased enrollments and admissions. Even though there were not many teachers, Beverly soon became the favorite student of every teacher who taught her.

"Excuse me, miss? Miss?" a male janitor stood beside Beverly, waiting for her to remove her foot from his mop. Zoned out, she gulped down some water, apologizing to the janitor before exiting the hall.

The classes commenced with Beverly attempting her best to stay awake and attentive. In most school days, attending chess and drama club meetings and events was her sole motivation. As she grew, she mastered the game of chess, winning titles and medals for her school… of course, none of that pleased Genevieve and Christian Miller.

As the final bell rang, Beverly gathered her things, feeling a sense of accomplishment and anticipation that were clearly overpowered by the need to take a nap. Walking home from the school bus stop, the thoughts about the awaiting household chores clouded her mind and blurred away her excitement about getting an A+ in most subjects.

That evening, at the dinner table, Beverly mustered up some courage to tell her parents about her achievement, "Momma, I got an A+ in Science, English, and Mathematics."

Genevieve continued munching on her salad, "Teddy, did you get to learn about more numbers?"

"Mhm…" spitting the mashed potato from his mouth, Teddy responded, "more numbers 10, 20, 50."

Beverly smiled, "That's great, Teddy. If you can't remember, just tell Beverly at night, and we will revise the lesson in no time."

"Finish up. You have to clean the table as well," Genevieve reprimanded.

Beverly stared at Genevieve, feeding a spoonful of vegetables to Teddy with brooding eyes. Christian ruffled Teddy's hair, kissed him good night, and headed to his study, instructing Beverly to bring him his cup of tea after dinner.

One knock, two knocks, three knocks, "May I come in?" the doorknob clicked, announcing Beverly's presence at Christian's study room door.

"If it is the tea, then yes; if not, then no," Christian hinted at his unavailability for any triviality.

"It is the tea," Beverly closed the door behind her and placed the teacup on a coaster on the study table.

"Dad, if you allow, can I ask a question?" Beverly stood with a serving tray held close to her chest.

"Just one, okay. What is it?" Christian continued scribbling something in the accounts book with reading glasses resting on the bridge of his nose.

"When we have house help, why do I do the chores?" Beverly spoke meekly.

"The house help is for your mother, and she decides what she wants them to do. Understood?" Christian looked at her from the top of his reading glasses, "Anything else?"

"Yes, does Momma love me?" Beverly looked down at the floorboards, fixating on the dust specks.

"Listen, Beverly, I really don't have time for this. There are other important stuff to worry about than this. Close the door behind you," Christian sipped on his tea as Beverly exited the study room and resumed her daily chores.

In her room's seclusion, Beverly found solace in doing voluntary work for school clubs and doing assignments for her teachers. In this family of four, loneliness became Beverly's companion, always there, mornings, nights, and evenings. The emptiness, inside and out, raged on, turning her existence into an echo chamber, reverberating the realities she wanted forgotten.

She took her test sheets, a golden star, and a big, red 'A' curved her lips into a smile. She quickly gathered her test sheets, fixed the bedsheet, and exited her room. Contemplating the thought of showing it to her mom, she halted in the middle of the hallway. *What if she scolds me? What if she wanted more than A? But there's nothing more than A… what if I don't show her, and she never asks? No, no, I should.* Forcing a smile and fortifying her teetering grit, Beverly headed towards her mother's room.

One knock. "What is it?" Genevieve hinted at her annoyance.

"I wanted to show you something. May I come in?" With one hand on her ear, Beverly held the test sheets tighter to her chest.

"Beverly? Is that you? Don't you know you are supposed to go to bed immediately after your chores. Why are you still up? I don't want any excuses for waking up late tomorrow morning and delaying the chores! Understand? Now, go to your room," Christiain's mutterings to calm Genevieve down were audible but incomprehensible.

"Okay, Momma," Beverly whispered her disappointment in a shaky voice.

The damp test sheets and the now half-erased, big, red 'A' cleared out her disillusionment with pleasing her parents. She returned to working on a project that a grade one teacher asked her to help with. The title of the project mocked her, literally: My Loving Mother.

Mothers, the angels on Earth, says the title of the project. The stenciled letterings deepened the sorrow, "I miss you, Ma," came out in the quivering words.

Mothers feed you, play with you, put you to sleep... she quickly wiped away the tears not to wet the project papers the teacher provided. She capped the pen, roughly dragged her sleeve on her eyes, and took out her stationery to add a creative flair to the project.

Following the teacher's instruction and penning down all that she provided, holding back the waterworks turned out to be a chore — something she was tired of.

Don't put the mothers to test,

They are not like the rest.

When all's bad,

Only mothers remain the best...

Beverly put a hand on her mouth, stifling her maddening woes. Knowing even the slightest of groans could intensify her dilemma, she took her pillow and cried into it. The only place children shouldn't be allowed is a house where they are forced to silent cry at hours the world sleeps.

Putting aside the idea of adding her creativity, Beverly quickly wrote the wordings in the color-coded manner as instructed. Lying on the ground with her pillow, she ventured on to fall asleep at a decent hour.

The next morning, Beverly was a picture-perfect example of sorrow-contained: baggy eyes, disheveled hair, chewed-down nails. However, her pitiful condition didn't cast a gloom on Genevieve's heart as her list of chores continued lengthening.

"Psst... Psst..." Teddy snapped his two fingers near Beverly's ear, peeling her away from the sluggish stupor.

"Teddy, I am working. Dishes aren't done," Beverly spoke under her breath, trying not to attract Genevieve's attention.

"I have something to show you," Teddy gestured her to quicken her pace.

Teddy's room was a domain of its own. With walls painted a soft gray, a neutral backdrop for the posters and ornaments that adorned them. Above the bed, a large frame of Christian, Genevieve, and Teddy smiling as a family added to the collection. Below it, a shelf lined with trophies and medals gleamed in the soft light – sports and academics – each a testament to Teddy's varied interests.

Near the window, a desk was piled high with schoolbooks, notebooks, and scattered drawings. A globe perched on one corner, while a set of pencils lay in a half-open drawer. The chair, though slightly too big for Teddy, where schoolwork was tackled. Right above the table a bulletin board held a collection of Teddy's family memories: photos of trips, ticket stubs from theme parks, and hand-drawn birthday cards by his mother — each pin held a story, a moment captured in time.

"Look at this!" Teddy held a wooden and alloy-made toy of a Boeing airplane painted in rustic golden, "Check this," he rotates the fan wings, and a whirring sound had the two kids awestruck.

"This sounds like a real one," Beverly carefully took the toy from her brother's hands and put her ear near its body to find out the source of sound.

"What if I can fly in it?" Teddy leaped on his bed, imitating the whooshing sounds of an airplane take-off.

"Haha, Teddy. No, you can't fly, but it is a good toy," Beverly placed it back on his desk.

"Beverly, will you play with me?" Teddy sat upright on the bed, puppy-eyed.

"I have chores, Teddy, and mother will be angry if I don't..." Beverly's excuses were met with Teddy's insistence.

"You never play with me. I don't feel like you are my sister." Teddy's long face changed Beverly's mind.

"Okay, only for a few minutes," Beverly ran in circles around Teddy's bed, emulating the movement and noise of an airplane.

Cackling, chasing, and tripping over the pillows, Teddy was a picture-perfect example of pure sibling joy. Beverly sprinted on her tippy-toes, whooshing the airplane higher than Teddy's reach.

"Ohh, here comes the big cloud," Beverly grabbed a fluffy white cushion, mouthed the noise of thunderbolts, and mimicked the sudden jolts and dips of airplane turbulence, her body swaying with imaginary bumps.

"Hold on tight!" she joked, her voice rising in mock alarm as Teddy clutched her leg in a playful simulation of a turbulent flight. The room around the siblings transformed into a chaotic airplane flight, complete with dramatic arm flailing and gasps, as the two laughed at their theatrical performance.

Beverly lowered the white cushion, a signal for Teddy to release her leg from his grip. "My turn! My turn!" Teddy jumped on the bed. Beverly leaped down the bed with an excited Teddy on her pursuit.

"Beverly!" the angered tone silenced the siblings' playful simulation, "Were all your chores done? I still see the dishes lying around the sink. The dust still covers the furniture… were all your chores done?" gritting her teeth, Genevieve dragged Beverly out of Teddy's room, smacking the door close.

Pulling her arm, Genevieve thrashed Beverly on her bed. Before Beverly could get a chance to regain her composure, Genevieve's spank had her clasping onto the bedsheet.

"HOW MANY…" came a sudden snap of a taut rubber band, "TIMES DO I…" then came a quick pop of a whip slicing through air, "TELL YOU TO…" this time, the sharp, stinging crack made Beverly wail, "DO YOUR CHORES!" then there was a lingering echo that seemed to hang in the room. Stifling her sobs left Beverly with ringing in the ears and benumbed backsides. The tirade of verbal abuse continued for an hour or so, punctuated with jerking and pushing Beverly's already numbed body. With her eyes cast

27

down following the confused tread of a tiny insect, Beverly nodded her head to the implications.

"I have tried over and over again to actually like you. You know, if you can just behave, I may even develop some love for you…but no, you have to ruin everything… just like your father!" Genevieve marched out of Beverly's room, leaving behind unresolved bewilderment.

Just like my father…what did dad do? Beverly lay on the bed on her stomach, *but dad is also Teddy's dad; why would she say 'your' father?* The tears raced down her face. *But… dad never bought me the airplane toy, and Teddy got it,* the questions inundated her young mind.

Beverly squirmed to the other end of her bed and grabbed a notepad and pencil from under the bed. The notepad tagged "Beverly's thoughts" opened to a doodle of Beverly standing hand-in-hand with her family. Inking the pages was her liberation from her forever unsettled mind.

~~Beverly in trouble~~

~~Beverly is sad~~

The Fuss

When bed time nears,

And to sleep you go,

There's always crying and

There's always a foe.

For little children love to stay,

And complete another day.

But mother's strict and lays the law,

So for children it's usually up the hall.

And into bed to go to sleep,

And when mother comes to peep

There the children are fast-asleep.

Sunday, the only day Christian Miller would spare some time to play with his children… that included Teddy and only Teddy. Even though Christian remained distant from Beverly, he never mistreated or disrespected her like Genevieve.

Beverly wished her mother a 'good morning,' excused herself from breakfast, and busied herself with the chores of the day. She started by dusting off the entire house, rubbing and scratching away any smut or grime. Smoothening the bedsheets, blankets, and pillow covers, she then proceeded to scrub under the kitchen sink. The foul smell of oil-covered drain pipes jeered at the sleep-deprived Beverly. The tiles under the sink presented another trial, with sludge blackening each corner.

She mixed the detergent with liquid soap and soaked the scrubber and sponge in that mixture. She took out the torch from the kitchen drawer and held it between her teeth. The torchlight helped her clean and scrub better.

"Beverly, have you done the gardens?" the question startled her, making her bump her head on the metallic sink.

Wiping the drool off her face from holding the torch, she garbled her response, "Nooo, I don…time."

"Did you or did you not?" Genevieve crossed her arms and raised a brow.

Gulping, emerging from under the sink with sludge on her face, "No, mother, I have not," Beverly awaited another series of expletives.

"Go, do it now. Teddy and Dad will play there for a while. C'mon," Genevieve clapped her hands twice, signifying the urgency of the said task.

Beverly dried the scrubbed tiles and headed outside to the garden. The mower started with a jolt, injuring Beverly's foot. Paying no heed to the wound, Beverly gathered the dried leaves, fallen fruits, and flowers and trashed them. She pruned the larger branches of the plants while rearranging the pots to ensure each one consumed sufficient sunlight. The last task in her garden work was to water the trees and plants.

The afternoon sun cast a warm glow as Beverly stood near the rows of pots and plants, watering them with a thick, yellow hose. She tiptoed from one plant to the next, her brow furrowed in concentration as the hose continued to slip from her grip. Making sure not to leave puddles near pots, Beverly took an easy-to-handle can, filled it with the streaming water from the hose, and watered each plant.

Behind her, bursts of laughter filled the air. Christian and her brother were engaged in an impromptu soccer match on the other side of the garden. Teddy sprinted across the lawn, his small legs pumping as he tried to dodge their dad, who playfully lunged to steal the ball. Every so often, Beverly would glance over her shoulder, watching them with a smile, before returning to her task.

Beverly coiled the hose, placed it back into the garage, and joined his brother and Christian, "Dad, can I play?" Beverly limped on one leg, trying not to put pressure on the injured one.

"Yes, Dad, Beverly is my team," Teddy's excitement brought about a fleeting but wide smile on Beverly's face.

"Beverly, have you done all the tasks your mother asked you to do?" Christian rubbed his forehead and rolled his eyes, avoiding any eye contact with Beverly.

Beverly nodded, exchanging a confused look with her brother. Disregarding Teddy's persistence, Christian enumerated the tasks assigned to her as Beverly shook her head in 'yes' and 'no.'

"What about those peonies at the motel? How many did you sell?" With one hand on his waist, Christian raised an eyebrow to show his contempt.

"I didn't sell all; some died," Beverly spoke in hushed tones with eyes cast down.

"Good for nothing. Now, I have to bear the loss of it. Go back inside and make yourself useful," Christian crossed his arms in front of his chest, showcasing his suppressed vehemence.

Wiping the tears with the back of her hand, Beverly halted near the house threshold, catching her breath and swallowing the sudden burst of emotions. Tears were just another excuse for Genevieve to insult Beverly. *Emotions aren't something kids supposed to understand or have*, she would often say this to her after every beating, admonishment, or any severity inflicted.

A few nights after, as assigned, Beverly was on her last chore of the day: serving tea to Christian in his study. Beverly knocked thrice, turned the doorknob, entered, and closed the door behind.

Bare-footed and with eyes focused on the wobbling teacup, Beverly tiptoed towards her father and set the cup on his table. Peeling the hangnails of her hands behind her back, Beverly chewed on her lips.

Christian took the first sip, a soft slurp followed by a brief hiss. He peeled his eyes away from his paperwork, took off his glasses, and restored the quill back into its holder. He pushed his chair back a bit, stood up, and picked up the teacup. "Drink this," he said.

"Can I get you another cup?" Is the tea okay?" Beverly spoke in a shaky voice; the hangnails were now abrasions.

"Drink this," the tone was stricter, the teacup now closer to her chewed-up lips.

Beverly took the cup from his hands and sipped on his tea, the heat burning the abraded lips, "The tea is still hot."

"Drink again," Christian demanded, now pacing around Beverly, glaring.

Beverly took a longer sip, swishing the tea before gulping it. "The sugar is fine. The tea is not too sweet." Hands trembling like a lonely leaf in a thunderstorm.

"Drink again, Beverly," Christian spoke with a hint of scorn in his tone while browsing his bookshelf.

Beverly took another sip, almost finishing the whole cup. Her lips now numbed to the burning sensation, "I am sorry. I will get you another cup."

Beverly's exit from the study was interjected with a sudden pull on her arm, followed by a resounding ring in her ear and a surging ache on her cheek. Beverly corrected her posture, letting the tears trickle down her chin and isolating the fear and shock.

"Get me tea with more tea leaves, understand? More tea leaves... a better cup of tea. Tell that to the house help and don't show your face again. Now get out!" Christian returned to his paperwork, leaving Beverly nailed to the ground in a state of shock.

"Father, I am sorry, but I did add enough tea leaves," Beverly sniffled.

"I am not your father! Just leave! Do I have to demonstrate that as well!?" Christian screamed the instructions, stripping her out of the shock.

The night revealed something Beverly wouldn't have realized otherwise: Beverly was not Christian Miller's daughter, nor was she ever loved by her mother.

The night marking the beginning of her twelfth year presented her with the gift of constant dilemma, never-ending despondency, and ever-strengthening anxiety.

***

The airplane became a fascination for Teddy. He used to sleep with it, take it to school with him, and narrate his creative stories about his plane to Genevieve — surprisingly, those stories held more importance than Beverly's expression of her emotions. One morning, he woke up to the plane's broken wing. Aware of what consequences his silliness could bring, Teddy was clever enough to sneak into Beverly's room and hide it under her bed.

"Mom, I cannot find my plane!" his pretense was flawless: a worried expression and tearful eyes.

"It must be in your room, dear," Genevieve consoled with an embrace.

33

"It isn't. I looked everywhere, and it isn't in my room," the trickle-down of a few tears had his mother in panic, throwing cushions in the living room and disrupting the furniture of the entire house.

"Where did it go, dear?" the well-scripted mystery had Genevieve scratching her head.

"We didn't check Beverly's room," Teddy added, smiling at the manifestation of his set plan.

"BEVERLY! BEVERLY!" Genevieve jolted the sleeping Beverly up.

"What happened?" Beverly, wide-eyed, wiped the drool off her mouth.

"Where's Teddy's plane?" Genevieve demanded answers.

"I don't know," Beverly responded, gulping on her dry mouth.

"Don't lie! I saw you in my room the other day," Teddy spoke, quivering.

"I didn't take the plane," Beverly got off the bed and corrected her clothes.

"I need to check your room," Genevieve scattered her handful of clothes on the floor, emptied the drawers of her necessities, and asked her to lift the mattress and move the bed to check under it. The broken plane lay there, deriding Beverly. Teddy snickered, content.

Genevieve tilted her head, feigning disappointment, "Of course, why would you not tell me the truth? Can't stand that Teddy is a better kid than you!"

Beverly felt her chest tightening. Over the years, Teddy realized he was untouchable as long as his lies were planned properly and the truth remained uncovered. He had made sure Beverly knew her place—beneath him. He wore his parents' affection like armor, and whenever he stumbled, whenever he made a mistake, he was quick to hurl the blame her way, knowing they would never question him.

Most of the time, Beverly was scolded for Teddy's lies, but the broken plane turned out to be a double sin: lying and ruining Teddy's stuff. This time, Genevieve made sure Teddy remained in the room when Beverly was belted.

The silence that followed was suffocating. Beverly stood, her legs trembling beneath her as she fought to hold back her sobs. She wanted to scream, to tell them everything, but the words stuck in her throat. No matter what she said, no matter how many times she begged them to listen, they never believed her.

She cast one last glance at Teddy, who stood with his arms crossed, a triumphant glint in his eyes. His smirk returned. She knew she would be locked in again, isolated and alone, while Teddy carried on, untouched by his lies.

The door to her room clicked shut, sealing her in her quiet prison. She sank to the floor, burying her face in her hands. The tears came then, silently, because loud cries had never helped her before. In this house, only silence was heard.

In the twelve years of her life, she lost what she knew was hers and ceased pursuing what she thought could be hers...

...the metamorphosis

The Good Shepherd Convent, Omaha, Nebraska, was a large, historic brick building constructed in the late 19th or early 20th century. The construction reflected the Gothic Revival and Romanesque architectural styles — typical of religious institutions. Featuring tall arched windows and a symmetrical façade, the central chapel with a bell tower stood out. The red and brown-bricked exterior with stone accents housed the vast grounds, green lawns, lush gardens, and pathways, evoking a sense of peace and reflection. Inside, the Convent had high ceilings, wooden pews in the chapel, and simple but spacious rooms for the sisters.

October 3, 1952, marked the day of Beverly's life away from Genevieve's house — emphasis on Genevieve's. That day singled out the fact Beverly had denied for years: there was no home for Beverly Ann Miller. Her grandparents loved her, but not enough to give her an assuring home. Her mother loved her conditionally... or was it just an obligation she wanted to be done with? Her father had always been a stranger to her — explains his awkwardness.

Where could my real father be? Does he know I am his daughter? What if he abandoned me as well? Will I ever meet him? The thoughts suffocated. With a mind filled with questions and tired eyes, Beverly started the first day at the Convent. The classes proceeded, and the eager students had their concerns resolved except for Beverly. She stared outside the window, watching the sun slowly set, casting shadows across the room. And in those shadows, her mind drifted to the face of a man she had never seen, a stranger who was somehow so important to who she was.

Was it mother's protection not to confuse me?

"She never loved you, Beverly. I never felt protected," she voiced the soliloquy.

Why didn't Grandpa and Grandma say anything?

"They don't love you, Beverly. Like mother, they only wanted you for their good," the shuddering sobs made her inconsolable.

What if my real father hates me, too?

"Everybody hates you, Beverly. You are to be hated..." she got up from the paper-thin mattress of her dorm bed and stood in front of the cracked mirror on the adjacent wall. Smeared with ink, stained by tears, a face she no longer recognized stared back at her. Remembering the ink and quill practice in one of her classes, she began rubbing her hands with a dirty cloth under her bed. The tears eased the hand cleaning.

"I am not loved.... Ma, Pa, you never loved me... nobody..." Beverly mumbled, brutally scraping her cuticles until they bled.

Her outburst was witnessed and reported by one of the cleaning ladies and an employed nun. The Convent suggested and initiated reformation classes for Beverly Ann Miller in aspects of maintaining her sanity and restoring her back to society. The reformation could take months or even years if the cooperation isn't reciprocated. Beverly welcomed puberty in the Convent and experienced the peaks of it during the Convent's reformation classes. The purpose was simple: reprogram the minds of the wayward.

Screaming imprecations, belting, and never-ending pressure to 'self-expel' the evil in yourselves — the evil of thinking for yourself was successfully exorcised. The reformed Beverly left the Good Shepherd Convent after 14 months with a note from the 'polite' nuns to let Beverly meet her real father.

When Beverly, an adolescent, returned home from the Convent, the Millers sold the motel on September 27, 1952, and moved to

Lincoln. Genevieve received the note from the Convent and went to Beverly's new room in Miller's new home.

Beverly's new room was smaller than the previous one, with space sufficient for a single bed and a dresser; all her clothes were still in the suitcase she had brought back from the Convent. *There's no need for a cupboard for you, and you will be going to a new school anyway,* Genevieve reasoned.

"So, you wanted to meet your real father, didn't you?" Genevieve walked around the small bed in Beverly's room, "Do you want this, or did someone tell you about him? I mean, he isn't that great of a man. The poor dullard."

"I wanted to meet him, mother," Beverly spoke, chewing on her nails.

"He is not that good of a man if that's what you are hoping for. Never respected your mother or my wishes," Genevieve rolled her eyes, threw her head backwards, and sat down next to Beverly on her creaking bed.

"He never wanted us, Beverly..." the bred creaked as she shifted positions, "he will never keep you happy as he never did me..." two consecutive creaks, "Everett Martin is no man to live with. You understand..." the creaks made Genevieve pound a couple of punches on the thin mattress as she ended up hurting her knuckles. The shriek of pain was followed by a sharp hit on Beverly's face and vituperation. Rage, confusion, loss — all tangled together, smothering her.

The ride from Genevieve's home to Everett's was a few hours long. Her stomach in knots, mind brimmed with queries, and heart pounded in a deafening rhythm. This was her day, the moment, the man she had imagined so many times but never actually known: Everett Martin.

Her legs felt shaky as she stood and gripped the strap of her bag. The cool air hit her face and brought a flush to her cheeks. She scanned the exterior of Everett Martin's house, looking for him.

And then she saw him.

He was standing by a rusted old pickup truck, leaning against it with his hands in his pockets. He looked older than she had imagined—his hair was gray at the temples, and his face was lined with years of hard living. But his eyes... his eyes were the same as hers. She froze for a second, her feet unwilling to move, taking him in. There was something familiar about him, even though he was a stranger. She swallowed hard, feeling the weight of the moment press down on her. Everett Martin took a step closer but still kept his distance as if unsure whether to come any closer.

Beverly shifted on her feet, the weight of all the questions she had been holding onto suddenly feeling too heavy to carry. "Why didn't you…"

"I never thought…I never knew….you are my daughter… you really…." he stopped himself, shaking his head.

Everett let out a slow breath and nodded, stepping a little closer, kneeling, and taking both her hands in his. "I'm glad I got to see you," he paused, heaved a sigh, and smiled, "You have no idea how glad."

"C'mon, now we have to head back. You met him. Now you behave," Genevieve pulled on Beverly's arms and dragged her back to the car, "We have to be home before sundown," she slammed shut the car door. Beverly remained glued to the window glass long after

Everett's house was out of sight — absorbing, processing, cherishing the only moment she ever felt a fatherly presence.

A few days later, Genevieve presented Beverly with a piece of paper titled "RESTRAINING ORDER." Genevieve explained to her the technicalities of a restraining order, expecting nothing but servility.

"I told you about this so that you don't ask me to take you there again… I really don't like that man," Genevieve began, tracing her steps back from the threshold of Beverly's room.

Why did she do this? The question throbbed in her chest, pulsing through every thought. It was only days ago that she'd met him—Everett Martin—her real dad. Her biological father. She had hoped, in her deepest heart, that meeting him would fill the void she never quite understood before.

And then—just like that—it was gone. All of it. He was gone. Genevieve had made sure of it. Beverly bit her lip so hard she tasted blood. *A restraining order.* It felt like her mother had ripped her heart out of her chest and stomped on it, leaving Beverly gasping for something she couldn't name. She had only seen him once, only spoken a few words, and now she would never see him again.

It was another way to control me, Beverly had her nails dug into her palm, the skin abraded, oozing blood. The conundrum had her peeling her hair out of her scalp.

"Now, now, you don't have to act up. I will let you process all this," Genevieve enveloped the notice.

"I. HATE. YOU, MOTHER! I HATE YOU!" The words thickened the discomforting silence between the two. Soon, the slashes of a leather belt replaced the silence interspersed by hoarse shrieks.

Sending Beverly to Convent was Genevieve's idea to fix her daughter's attitude and instill values of obedience and respect. Beverly had to change five schools, while her attitude remained inveterate. The strict routines and long hours of studying didn't amend the strong emotions she felt for her parents, especially Genevieve. After every few months, Beverly was sent back from the convent with a note declaring her 'too hard to handle' — some thought her to be possessed by an evil spirit, while others labeled her mentally unable to find God and peace.

The fourteen-year-old was sent back to her grandparents, Edna and Lloyd, in Arizona. The anger turned into perversity, leaving an untamed Beverly Ann Miller for Edna and Lloyd to take care of. Screaming imprecations, swearing by the Lord's name, thrashing the whole house, this Beverly was a stranger to them. The stay at her grandparents lasted less than half a year, and Beverly returned to Lincoln.

What her grandparents considered a fresh start felt like a cruel joke to Beverly. Her heart hardened with each accusation, each dismissal of her pain. She wasn't a liar. She wasn't incorrigible. She wasn't a bad student or a daughter. She was a girl who had been lied to for years, a girl who had been abandoned emotionally by the people who were supposed to love her.

*Too wild, too loud, but never enough...*Beverly sat with her bags in the lounge, awaiting her mother to take her to a new school.

"Leaving so soon?" Teddy chuckled, nibbling on a freshly made cookie. He flumped down on an adjacent couch, "You know, you should try to work on your behavior; it's really bad, like stinky bad. A bite?" He offered Beverly the cookie, but pulled away his hand before she could take a nibble. An acerbic farewell was the last she heard of her half-brother.

*Maybe I am troubled, maybe I am the bad person...maybe if I run away far, far away, I will no longer have problems...*Beverly peeked from the hallway towards her parents' room. Apparently, her mother was still indecisive about the dress to wear to her new school. The trivialities have always been Genevieve's priorities.

Walking on her toes with one bag on each shoulder, Beverly placed her luggage near the main entrance and, with gliding steps, went back to check on her mother. Genevieve had the door locked now – Beverly's signal to leave or stay.

How do you keep going when no one wants you around? How do you keep loving people who only see you as a mess they need to fix? The doorknob clicked. A chill breeze blew in.

*They sent me to different schools because they don't want anything to do with me... it is better if I just vanish...*Beverly lifted her two bags and wrapped the neck scarf a bit tightly.

How bad could the world be to me when my own family has disowned me, another click, and Beverly had crossed the cobblestone pathway and turned the corner.

On November 15, 1955, Genevieve decided to wear a sophisticated, fawn color dress designed by the town's famous seamstress to Beverly's new convent school.

Maybe I'm just destined to be this girl—this version of myself, Beverly zipped her jacket up to the neck. Genevieve called for Beverly, struggling to put in her earrings.

I can't stay there and wait for the good days. No one's coming for me. Not Mom. Not Dad. Not anyone, Beverly took out another pair of socks, put it on, and laced her shoes tightly in hopes of keeping her feet warm. Genevieve trotted in her heels from room to room, screaming her daughter's name.

Maybe there's a better place for me. Maybe the next school. Or maybe it's just all the same. Maybe I am fated to suffer, Beverly wended her way to the nearest store to shelter herself from the breeze. Genevieve grabbed her fur coat and exited the house, ordering the driver to bring about her vehicle.

But I can't do what they want. I was betrayed; I was lied to, Beverly reached the closest bus stop and, a while later, hopped on the next bus with no destination in mind. Genevieve reprimanded the driver for not being watchful of her incorrigible while looking outside the car window.

But I'm not allowed to be anything, right? I'm not allowed to ask for more. More love, more truth, more… anything … not in this life that was never meant for me.

On November 21, 1955, Beverly was found. The rumor had it that she was at the Air Base with someone. Maybe she was, maybe she wasn't. But she returned to be branded as the girl of the streets by her biological mother and stepfather. The girl of the streets was sent to yet another high school, only to be strengthened in her rebellion.

Chapter 3: The Cycle Repeats

The high-school Beverly wasn't the kind of girl to shy away from disrupting classes, breaking rules, or even challenging boys. The timid, oppressed Beverly at the Millers' house was a loud, speak-my-mind type of high-schooler. Teachers tried to pretend they didn't notice, but everyone knew what Beverly stood for: she wasn't about to conform. Beverly Ann Miller didn't just break the rules; she *challenged* them, daring the world to stop her.

But rebellion wasn't the problem, at least not to Beverly. Rebellion was her survival in high school, her escape from high school bullying. It was how she fought back against a world that kept perceiving her as a problem to be solved. She rebelled because she needed to carve out a space for herself, somewhere she could breathe. The high school became her haven to let out her frustrations. Even after constant and strict complaints to her parents, Beverly remained firm in her perception — be bullied or become a bully.

Hence, the transfers from one high school to another. For the first time in almost decades, Beverly Ann Miller had her mother's and stepfather's attention. The abused was now domineering the abusers… or she thought so.

The constant pushing back, the fights with teachers and her parents, the realization of having no friends—it sometimes felt like she was caught in a storm she couldn't escape. And underneath all the rebellion, all the bravado, there was a small part of her that just wanted to be understood and loved, completely and absolutely.

The walk from her house to high school was when the timid, submissive Beverly transformed into a reckless, uncontrolled teenager — which is why Genevieve never understood the reason behind the complaints about her insolence. Wearing her regular-fit t-shirt and loose trousers, Beverly weaved her way to the bus stop to get on her assigned school bus.

"AHHH!" she smacked the metallic pole, seeing no empty seats, "Every time! Why can't these oldies walk to work? At least their bones won't crack and creak that much," she spoke under her breath, but loud enough to be heard by a teenager standing beside.

Beverly gathered her backpack and headed towards the front side of the bus stop when a mutter made her turn back, "What did you say?"

"I said if these oldies started walking, there wouldn't be anyone to call oldie, cuz they will want to be called young," the tall, dark-haired, with hazel eyes jested. His eyes glimmered with a sort of delight that excited Beverly.

Putting his hand out for introduction, he said, "I am Melvin Hess. I am from North Carolina, and yes, out of high school. Jeez, that place, my condolences," a smoldering stare, "and now in the military."

"Beverly Ann Miller, 17, hoping this school…" shrugging, "or life to end soon, whatever," Beverly stuck out her hand. His hand felt warm in her hardened palm. The house labor peeled away the softness of her teenage features and the warmth from her personality.

"That's wild, woman, life!? That wasn't expected," Melvin leaned back against the stop sign pole, hands in pockets.

"Who cares, whatever happens, happens for a reason," Beverly began walking towards the incoming bus, "Will see you around, got to be wild," doing air quotes, "in class as well."

There was nothing extraordinary about their first interaction — just an ordinary week day wrapped in the usual rush, traffic noises, and complaining students. He noticed the agony engulfing her, the unspoken anxiety. Even though the words exchanged were few, there was an unexpressed acknowledgment that Beverly couldn't quite name. Something had begun—quietly, subtly, but unmistakably real.

The lectures faded behind the reverberating introduction of Melvin. Her mind raced back to the hazel eyes, finding her nervous gaze to meet — this new stranger somehow acquired Beverly's determination to know him, an exception she just might make this one time.

Melvin soon captured Beverly's attention. Waiting for him in the morning before her bus became her routine. His gaze would remain on her only to be removed when Beverly left for school — there was a certain admiration, a hint of respect.

The morning chatters were replaced by late afternoon walks to their house. Melvin taking the opposite route, only to spend a few more minutes with Beverly, and Beverly taking the longest route to her house only to avoid her release from Melvin's gaze. Somehow, he brought out compassion in her; she was less loud, talked nicely, and was less angry. All the walls, the defenses she had built to protect herself, began to crumble quietly, piece by piece.

It was like finally coming home after wandering lost for years. That's how it felt—being understood, really understood, for the first time in what seemed like forever. It wasn't grand or dramatic; it was a steady, gentle recognition—a feeling that said, *I see you, all of you, and it's enough.*

The weight she had carried for so long, the fear of being misunderstood, of always being a problem, began to lift. It was peace. It was belonging. It was home – Melvin became her home. The homeliness lasted a few more months before Melvin was called to return to his military duties, and then there was the renascence of Beverly as a fearless, outspoken daughter.

"I will go to school when I want to!" Beverly snatched her backpack from Genevieve's hands, marching towards the room.

"You come right back here, Beverly! I am your mother, and you listen to me," Genevieve clenched her fists, cheeks crimson.

"Or what?" Beverly raised her finger at her.

"I will smack you. I had better not hear another complaint from your school. You heard me? Not one more!" Genevieve stomped to Teddy's room and cursed her daughter, with Teddy saying 'Amen' to every damnation.

Beverly only met Melvin for a little while after school before running back home to complete her chores. Melvin broke the news of possibly shifting to North Carolina to return to the military. The disclosure brought forth emotional and mental turmoil for Beverly. The seventeen-year-old suffered panic attacks and anxiety. Genevieve, unknowingly but pleased, would let her suffer, demanding more housework.

"Stop being dramatic," Genevieve said, her voice flat like this was just another inconvenience. "You've still got to clean out the dead plants," eyes narrowed with impatience with no hint of concern.

One fortunate day, while combating her anxiety attack, Beverly could only say one word to ease her nerves: Melvin. Genevieve heard the name and was quick to draw conclusions, accurate reckonings as to say.

"So, who is the lover boy, huh?" Genevieve towered over Beverly, crouching down to pick out the dead leaves.

"Who is…What!?" Beverly leaped to her feet, gripping the spade tightly.

"Don't you dare lie to me! Who's name were you mumbling while acting out? Tell me!" Genevieve snatched the spade and twisted one of Beverly's ears.

Squirming in pain, Beverly told her whole truth, "Melvin. We met at the bus stop. He is in the military and lives in North Carolina," Genevieve let go of her ear, "and is here to visit his relatives."

Smiling, Genevieve tucked the stray strand behind Beverly's reddened ear and cupped Beverly's face in her hand, "Oh, that's sweet. So, it was love at first sight? When will he go back to Carolina?"

Stepping away from her mother's sudden show of affection, Beverly hesitated, "He said he will go back in a couple of weeks…"

"Aw, that's sad. Oh, oh! Now I get it! This is why you were anxious all this time," patting Beverly's back, "You do love him that much?"

"Yes, I do," Genevieve looped her arm in Beverly's, forcing her daughter to walk around the lawn.

"So, you'd rather be with him not to be anxious and panicked, right?" Genevieve remarked, goading Beverly to react.

"Yes, of course. Why do you ask?" Beverly pulled away from her mother, brows furrowed.

"I ask because I want you to be with him…" Genevieve took an intentional pause, observing Beverly's reaction, "… so I could marry you off with him!" Genevieve twirled and clapped her hands, demonstrating her excitement.

"Really! Are you serious!? You will do that… you will?" Beverly embraced her mother as the two frolicked around jubilantly.

"I will talk to your dad and have the paperwork ready," Genevieve said, squeezing Beverly's hands.

"My dad…" Beverly held onto her mother's hands a bit tightly, expecting.

"Oh, forget that loser," Christian Miller was to appear as her father in Beverly's marriage processions.

August 17th, 1957, the courtroom was small, filled with the sharp smell of varnished wood and freshly printed paperwork.

A judge, an older man with stern eyes behind thin glasses, sat at the raised bench. To his left, the clerk had organized a thick stack of documents. At the center was Beverly, dressed in a plain, white, knee-length dress, smiling ear-to-ear. Next to her was Melvin, calm, almost too calm, wearing a crisp suit, stealing glimpses of his to-be bride.

The judge lifted his gavel lightly, then rested it back down. The soft thud silenced the murmurs.

"This is the matter of Beverly Ann Miller and Melvin Hess' application for the marriage certificate. Is this correct?" the judge spoke in a heavy baritone voice, peering from the top edge of his thin glasses.

Beverly nodded, smiling at Melvin, who had maintained a decent distance.

"Both of you understand the terms of this marriage?" the judge inquired, signing on the document.

Melvin stepped forward, his voice smooth and steady, and words practiced, "Yes, your honor. We do."

"It's always a little surprising to see such... efficiency when it comes to marriage. You're both aware of the legal commitment this entails?" the judge took off his glasses, placing them atop the papers.

"We are, your honor," Beverly spoke with a hint of urgency, fidgeting on her feet.

The Judge leans back in his chair, eyeing them both, "This union is recognized by the state. However, I must ask, is this arrangement made willingly by both parties?"

Melvin and Beverly, without missing a beat, chimed in with the same affirmative, "Absolutely."

The Judge studied their faces, his fingers tapping lightly on the bench. "Alright. If both parties agree, I'll proceed. Just be aware that marriage is more than a legal contract. It's a commitment."

He paused for effect, with Beverly and Melvin nodding in agreement. The clerk quietly handed over a document to the judge.

The judge asked the to-be-married couple to come forward. They approached the bench and bent down to sign their names. Beverly signed quickly, as though the pen was too heavy to hold. Melvin followed suit, his hand moving with calculated precision.

As they returned to their places, the Judge took a long, unblinking look at them one last time. He knew these kinds of marriages—convenience, necessity, or something else altogether. He offered a small, half-hearted smile.

"Congratulations. You're now legally married." He banged the gavel lightly.

Melvin leaned and landed a brief but unhurried kiss on Beverly's forehead, ensuring the families of the two weren't ill at ease. As they exited the courthouse, the air between them was palpable—a rescue-cum-marriage, a deliverance, a burden off the shoulders.

"Look at you, the prettiest bride!" Genevieve hugged and kissed her daughter, "Oh, you are so lucky, Melvin. I have trained her for everything: cleaning, cooking, grocery… you name it."

"That's great, Mrs. Miller," Melvin took Genevieve's extended hand and gave it a peck, "but I truly do love your daughter."

"Sure, you do," Genevieve pulled back her hand, wrapping it around Christian's arm, "she is surely now YOUR problem."

"We will come visit, right, Beverly?" Melvin caressed Beverly's knuckles as the two had their hands intertwined. Beverly locked eyes with Melvin, breathing a sigh as if all the worries began to melt. The gentleness of his touch, the quiet understanding in his eyes, was so far from the sharp, critical apprehension of her mother. The newlyweds were sent off in a black horse wagon embellished with white and red flowers and a handwritten label publicizing their marriage.

Tears welled in her eyes, not from sadness but from the sheer relief of it all. She was free, free to feel cared for, to feel worthy of something as simple and profound as tenderness.

Melvin let her rest her head on his shoulder. He didn't say anything. He didn't need to, as his presence was enough for Beverly to find peace. To her, it was like a quiet, steady anchor. In that ride to Melvin's residence, she had found something her mother had never given her: peace.

Beverly, 17 years old, finally bade farewell to the everyday harangue, comparison, and abjection. As she falls in love with the new awaited life, Beverly, for the first time in years, hoped... for goodness and goodness only.

***

The late evening sun cast a warm light over the small wooden house, nestled in a scarcely populated rural area of North Carolina. The house, painted a soft blue that had faded over the years, looked as though it had been plucked from an old postcard. It's front porch sagging ever so slightly, the paint peeling just enough to show the bare wood beneath.

Inside, the scent of fresh paint and wicked-off incense sticks mingled in the air. Beverly stood in the doorway, one hand resting on the weathered frame, her eyes scanning the room. She could hear distant sounds of barn animals and the occasional chirps of birds hidden in the tall trees. The place was small, much smaller than what she had imagined when Melvin mentioned his residence. But it was theirs—his inheritance and her home.

With one master bedroom, a smaller bedroom, a lounge, and a kitchen, Beverly's heels clapped as she took in the homeliness and familiarity of the house.

This is where Pa and Ma used to have tea together, her hands slightly grazed the head of the sofa in the lounge. Although small, Melvin's house had the furnishings set in the same manner as Edna and Lloyd's.

But why did they let me go back? Do they not love me anymore? Beverly's eyes welled up, bringing about the suppressed rage. *They also love mother more than me. They also think of me as a problem — I am nothing more than a problem...*

"Beverly, let's go. Allow me," Melvin's arm around Beverly's shoulder broke her train of thought as she quickly wiped the tears waiting to stream down.

"Hey, listen, it's okay to miss your family and cry. Don't stop yourself. If you want to cry and talk about them, we will do that. Okay?" Melvin gave her shoulders a slight squeeze, making her nod and sniffle.

The first few months in the little house were a whirlwind of discoveries, both about each other and about their new life together. Beverly and Melvin spent their days painting walls, fixing old windows, and purchasing kitchenware and wall decorations. Every project brought a challenge, and every challenge brought them closer.

Beverly would wake up at dawn break to start her day early and not miss any of the decided tasks for the day — old habits are indeed difficult to let go of. The routine made her admire the stillness of the house in those early hours, the way the light crept in slowly through the sheer curtains, painting the walls in soft shades of gold. She would brew coffee in the tiny kitchen with its old, unreliable stove and sit on the porch, watching the mist rise off the trees. By the time Melvin joined her, groggy but smiling, she'd have two mugs waiting, their hands brushing as they passed each other in the doorway.

Melvin would take on the heavier tasks—repairing the fence, fixing the electrical wiring, or digging out the stubborn tree roots in the garden. Beverly would watch him sometimes, marveling at how quickly her life had shifted from the anxiety of imitating perfection at her mother's house to the quiet routine of fixing up her home. But there was joy in it, in the mundane.

Their love blossomed in the small things, in the laughter shared over spilled paint or the quiet moments where words weren't necessary. At night, they'd collapse onto the old sofa, exhausted from the day's work. The house would be silent except for the sound of crickets outside.

"I think we can upgrade our garden... I mean, it is far from looking like an actual garden, but we can add some herbs, vegetables, or even fruit. What do you think?" Melvin planted a soft kiss on Beverly's forehead.

A sigh and a peck to Melvin's cheek, "Whatever you want as long as you go and shop for those seeds and plants."

"I don't know if I will be able to take proper care, so you will have to pitch in," Melvin said, pulling Beverly closer.

"Don't stress, you are good at everything you do," Beverly tilted her head to meet his eyes.

"Not everything," he replied, his voice dropping to a soft murmur as he ran his hand through her hair. "But I'll keep trying if it means I get to do it with you."

In the months that followed, their love deepened in ways neither of them could have predicted. They found joy in the simplest moments—cooking together, brewing coffee, sitting on the porch, and dancing in the rain. They learned each other's rhythms, routines, and quirks—how Beverly needed her plushie to sleep well, or how Melvin disliked folding his clothes and organizing his cupboard.

They laughed more, argued more, and loved more, but every argument seemed to end in Melvin pulling her into his arms, his lips brushing her temple as he whispered, "I love you, even when you don't agree with me."

Beverly would always smile, more in bewilderment and less in excitement because, deep down, she realized how, like every other good thing in her life, this marriage still felt like a dream.

As the house slowly transformed around them, so did their marriage, from the fiery passion of newlyweds to something strangely unfamiliar yet regretfully accustomed.

The Hess family of two was blessed with the good news of the addition of the third when, during the fourth month of pregnancy, Melvin received orders to go to Guam. For Beverly, the end of 1957 seemed like the end of her happy life.

The house grew quiet, a silence that could smother you. The hush inside the house brewed a storm inside her, cracking, raging, shattering her. She sat on the porch with a cup of coffee as insipid as her life. Tracing the taut skin of her stomach, she tightly closed her eyes, trying to erase his promises of returning, writing to her, and taking care of her — all the claims ring hollow in her ears.

The loneliness was unbearable, and the more she tried to push it away, the heavier it became, settling into her bones until she could barely move under the weight of it. *What if she is left on her own to take care of the baby? What if he isn't the faithful one? What if...* she heaved deep breaths, dropping and breaking the mug of coffee

— that was the sixth coffee mug forfeited for the sake of Beverly's anxiety.

The fourth month entered into the fifth, then the sixth. And by then, the silence began speaking to her. The seemingly solo utterances had invented a "Melvin" Beverly had befriended. She would talk and laugh at her imaginative Melvin. However, each night the lonesome sleep would remind her of his dreadful absence.

The desideration nourished desperation… and desperation is where extremity meets normalcy. The closer the delivery date gets, the stronger the desperation grew. Beverly didn't even realize when the thought entered her mind, but once it did, there was nothing else to consider. *If he loves you, he will never see you hurt. If you are hurt, he will run back home.* As twisted as it sounded, Beverly ended up giving into this logic and resorting to self-harm.

At first, it started with crying herself to the point where breathing ceased, but bravery wasn't what she had then. It proceeded with starvation, but the thought of taking an innocent life had her guzzling on multiple meals at a time. And then came the most dangerous of all: she gave up hope entirely. Her hands trembled as she reached for the small, sharp blade she had hidden in the drawer beside the bed. She stared at it for a long time, her heart pounding in her chest. She didn't want to die. She didn't want to leave this world without meeting her baby, without seeing Melvin again. But the fear, the aching loneliness—it was unbearable.

And this… this felt like the only option.

Mama, I love you, Mama… the voice of her unborn had kept company for the past few weeks. She imagined this time to be different, filled with pure joy and celebration of their first-ever baby. The tears wetted her swollen belly. Hiccupping, she, for the first time, saw her baby's kick.

Fidgeting the slim blade between the thumb and index finger, Beverly heaved audibly and waddled her way to the bathroom. *He will come back Beverly,* the idée fixe was now deep-rooted in her mind. She sat on the edge of the bathtub and turned on the tap, and the porcelain felt cool against her skin. The slushing water reached the brim, wetting Beverly's nightgown and puddling the floor. She felt another kick, stronger this time — a reminder of the life inside her, but not sufficient to keep her alive to birth or nurture another one.

Shutting the tiny voice of her baby in her mind, Beverly wailed, "You can bring back my Melvin; if you can't do that, I don't need you. I don't need anyone but Melvin..." collapsing to the flooded floor and pulling at her hair, "...I just need my Melvin, please."

Splashing the overflowing water on her face, she placed the slim blade on her wrist, hands trembling like a lonely leaf in a windstorm. The metal felt foreign on her skin, like an intruder awaiting the time to strike. The coldness of the blade was oddly familiar as a reciprocation to the numbness within. Beverly squeezed her swollen eyes shut; the world felt out of reach, the slushing water a miserere to her drowning self.

Holding her breath, Beverly pressed the blade a tad harder on her wrist. Jolting through her, the pain was sharp but unsurprising. Letting out a ragged and croaky sob, she pressed it harder, watching her skin tear under the object she determined to be her savior. The thick crimson bloomed, staining the nightgown, streaming down her bitten-down nails, and discoloring the white, immaculate tile Melvin had fixed.

She sat in the bloodied pool and, with a slashed wrist, placed the blade on the other wrist. In a swift slit and gurgling sound, her wrists bled out the despair Beverly had shouldered during this pregnancy.

"Melvin will come home," she repeated the obsessive trigger until another kick from the baby brought her out of the unconscious. Melvin's words reverberated in the place of her possible death: *I can't wait to see the baby. I dearly hope it looks just like you... my precious little Beverly.*

"No, no..." voice quavering and fumbling to get on her feet, Beverly dragged herself to the towel hanger and pulled down the hand and bath towels. She clumsily wrapped the towels on her slashed wrists, dragged her bloodied body towards the main door, and lost consciousness as the door lock clicked open.

Fortunately, one of the neighbors saw her lying outside and was quick to act and take her to the hospital. A call was made to Melvin, informing him of Beverly's condition. Melvin Hess arrived at the hospital a day later, waiting for her to regain consciousness. Melvin stayed for two weeks to ensure Beverly had recovered and was well enough to continue her daily chores. The slashes left long and deep scars on her wrists, a cruel reminder of what desperation could look like.

The first task that welcomed Melvin home was the bloodied and now-coagulated bathroom floor. Accredited to the warm weather, the dried-up blood in the bathroom had left a strong, metallic smell lingering throughout the Hess's home — *any place can only be a home when I have my Melvin with me.*

The flakiness of the dark brown coagulated blood turned scrubbing the floor into a hectic job. Wringing piece after piece of blood-soaked cleaning towels, Melvin stared at his crimsoned nail beds. His hands shivered, marginally with muscle ache and stiffness, and majorly with the starkness of it all. It was as if he could see it all unfold. The horror wasn't just in the act of cleaning—it was in the realization that no matter how hard he scrubbed, the memory of it would never fade. The floor might become clean again, but she would never be the same. The worst of all, Beverly didn't know Melvin's departure would be in a couple of days.

Melvin's return to Guam encountered a sobbing, hiccupping Beverly, tugging at her blanket and using the hem of it as her handkerchief.

"Do you have to go, Melvin?" Beverly pulled at Melvin's sleeve, wrists still aching because of the laceration.

"Bev, it is important too. How will I put bread and butter on the table if I am to stay?" Melvin, seated on the bed's edge, cupped Beverly's face and gently caressed it. She clung to him tighter as if her embrace could stop the inevitable. His hands loosened around her; she had her eyes squeezed shut as if memorizing his warmth, scent, heartbeat… his presence. A peck on the forehead and he was gone, leaving her to her miserable self.

On July 20th, 1958, Jodie Lynn Hess was born. She was a healthy baby with the face of her father and hair similar to her mother. The bundle of bliss she risked to bring back Melvin somehow became the orbit of Beverly's existence. Beverly was now a fully grown adult of 18 years of age, and Melvin was 20. Melvin returned, once again, to meet his first-ever child, a daughter. The new parents bedecked their room with tinsels, toys, and balloons, and welcomed their benediction with gratitude and love.

Since his birth, Melvin frequented his visits to spend any and every time as he could find with his daughter. Their room was now a nursery, playground, and whatever little Jodie wanted it to be.

The house was different now, almost unrecognizable in its transformation. Where once there had been stillness and quiet, an air of serenity that settled in the rooms like dust, now there was movement, noise, and a hum of life that never truly stopped.

The living room, once a space of neatly arranged furniture and calm, now bore the unmistakable signs of upheaval. Soft toys were scattered like forgotten thoughts, colorful and bright against the muted tones of the rug. The once-spotless iron stand was now a makeshift diaper station, wipes, and creams tucked haphazardly into baskets. Bottles and pacifiers seemed to appear everywhere, as though they multiplied in the chaos.

The kitchen, too, had changed. The fridge door was covered in magnets holding up baby photos and reminder notes that seemed to increase by the day. The smell of baby food often lingered, sweet and strange, blending with the aromas of home-cooked meals.

It was harder now, messier, noisier. But there was something in the air that hadn't been there before—a kind of warmth, a hum of life. The house had changed after the baby, but so had Beverly. It wasn't just a place to live anymore; it was a place where something precious grew, learned, and filled every corner with the sound of possibility. In fact, the transformation wasn't just of the house but of Beverly's purpose, too.

The little one proved to be a bandage to the weakening relationship between Beverly and Melvin, even though Melvin's visits weren't often anymore. Little Jodie was 10 months old, nearing her first birthday, when a phone call brought back what Beverly never thought to encounter again: Genevieve Miller.

"This is the North Carolina Police Department. Is this Beverly Ann Hess, wife of Melvin Hess?" the voice spoke in a strict tone.

"Yes, I am Beverly," she replied in a shaky voice.

"Is Genevieve Miller your mother?" the question had Beverly conflicted.

"Yeah… she is," Beverly confirmed hesitantly.

"We called to inform you about your mother, Genevieve Miller; she hasn't been well lately and has asked for you to come," the officer paused for her to respond.

"Okay, why?" Beverly tightened her grip on the phone receiver, knuckles turning white.

"As I said, she isn't well and has been sick. We are asked to summon you and your husband, Melvin Hess, to Nebraska. We hope she recovers and lives a long life. Have a good day, Mrs. Hess," the line went dead.

Beverly took a seat on the couch with her face buried in her hands. She wanted to be a good daughter, to care for her mother as she aged, but the memories of past cruelties flashed through her mind, sharp and unrelenting. She longed for her daughter to meet her grandmother, to build some connection. But she couldn't help but wonder, *to what end? What kind of relationship could truly grow from a legacy of hurt?* The cackling interrupted her train of thought, only to meet the smiling, drooling face of little Jodie.

"Oh, what should mama do?" Beverly gathered her in her arms, rocking and tickling little Jodie. The uncontrolled laughter erased Beverly's apprehensions, though momentarily.

"She sure is in a good mood, right?" Melvin took Jodie from Beverly's arms, blowing a raspberry on Jodie's stomach, followed by her snorting and chuckling breathlessly.

"Genevieve is sick," Beverly spoke in a rather serious tone, drawing all of Melvin's attention.

"How do you know? She called? She never had our number," Melvin handed Jodie a rattle to keep her amused.

61

"The North Carolina Police Department called to inform us that she had summoned us because of her sickness," Beverly pressed her temple, heaving a nervous sigh.

"What do you want? I will do whatever you think is right; it should be your decision," Melvin pulled at her arm, motioning her to sit and relax.

"Should I go? I mean, Jodie never got to meet her grandmother," Beverly kissed Jodie's hands, smiling at the drooling baby.

"Pfft... grandmother," Melvin spoke, words dripping with sarcasm.

"The officer said Chris had sent out a money order of $75 to afford our traveling expenses, too," Beverly informed, taking Jodie and heading towards the kitchen sink to clean Jodie's face.

A week later, the Hess family was on the bus to have Jodie meet her grandmother for the first time. The money Chris Miller sent turned out to be more than sufficient for their two-way travel. The bus rattled along the highway, carrying a handful of passengers from North Carolina to Nebraska. The landscape outside had shifted from rolling hills to flat, empty plains. The entire ride, Jodie remained in her mother's arms. The gentle rocking of the bus lulled her into drowsiness.

Nearing Nebraska, Beverly's anxiety peaked. Sensing the change in body language, Melvin wrapped his arm around her shoulders. She promised herself never to return to Genevieve's house, yet there she was, headed right towards it with her family. No matter how Genevieve treated her, for Beverly, she was the only family Beverly could rely on—the cruelty isn't the mistreatment but the uncompromisable bond.

The cab came to an abrupt halt, jolting Beverly up from her nap. Little Jodie remained fast asleep, wrapped in her soft blanket, snuggled against her mother's chest. The Victorian elegance that once had welcomed her to a new home has now become a place she dreads. In all its vastness, the freshly ivory-painted structure symbolized a prison she escaped.

"So, this was the correctional facility you grew up in?" Melvin jested and was nudged by Beverly on his right arm.

Putting an arm on her shoulder, he continued, "Relax, she is sick. I don't think she'll be able to scold you much." Beverly exhaled and forced a smile.

Melvin struck the brass knockers twice; the clattering woke Jodie up, only to be put back to sleep with Beverly's rocking. Melvin knocked on the door again, a bit louder now, "What if they went to the hospital? I mean, your mother could be seriously sick."

"No, they usually take longer to answer doors if I am not at home. I guess they don't bother about the visitors," Beverly said under her breath to ensure Jodie remained asleep.

"Alright, alright! I am coming. God, why do you have to be so impatient? Who is it?" Teddy's guttural voice made a complaining welcome of his half-sister. The adolescent half-brother stood agape at the threshold, eyes scrutinizing the first-time mother.

"Why are you here?" Teddy, in a swift motion, pushed the door, leaving it half-open.

"I am here to meet Genevieve," Beverly pushed her way inside, brushing past Teddy's shoulder, and Melvin followed.

"Mother, I am here. How are…" Beverly halted in her tracks, turning pale as she saw her mother sitting in the lounge with her friends and playing cards with a wine goblet dangling from her hand.

"Beverly…" Genevieve set down the glass and cards on the table. Beverly forced a smile and uttered "hello" through clenched teeth.

"Friends, this is my daughter, Beverly. Beverly…" Genevieve turned her gaze towards her, and like clockwork, Beverly knew what was required. She went around the table, hugging and greeting mother's friends.

"What made you visit us, Beverly?" Genevieve and her friends resumed the game, disregarding Beverly's presence in all.

"I heard you were sick and that you requested my presence here," Beverly spoke reluctantly, gesturing for Melvin to hold Jodie.

"I am not sick! Do I look sick, or do you want me to be sick? That's really rude of you, young lady," Genevieve clucked her lips, picking up a card from the deck.

"I don't mean it that way. I apologize if it came off that way. we came all this way because we were summoned BY you, and thought MAYBE…" Beverly caressed Jodie's cheek, her gaze searching her mother's slightest glimpse, "you wanted to meet your new granddaughter since you were ill."

"So? She is your problem, Beverly…" Genevieve raised her brows, pointed at Melvin, and smirked, "just as she is yours."

Melvin mouthed to Beverly, "Let's go," and excused himself to get a cab for their departure. Beverly stifled a sob and addressed Genevieve, "Mother, I came here, all worried for you. But now I know that you don't need me… at all."

"Bevs, I never did, and God forbade if I ever did," Genevieve waved away Beverly's hushed sobs and continued with the game.

Beverly's mind replayed every moment of her childhood, every cold dismissal, every sharp word, every torment bestowed upon her. This wasn't new. This was Genevieve—calculated, cold, always in control. But somehow, it still hurt just as much as it did when Beverly was a girl. She had thought becoming a mother herself might bridge the chasm between them, that Genevieve might finally see her not as a disappointment but maybe as an acquaintance if not a daughter. Instead, she had been reminded—cruelly and unmistakably—that Genevieve's love was something she would never earn.

"Goodbye, mother. I should leave now," Beverly exited the lounge of Miller's house without any blessing… the same way she was married off to Melvin.

As the cab pulled up, Beverly climbed in with Jodie nestled in her arms. The Millers' house, with its desolate opulence and even colder occupants, faded behind them. For the first time, Beverly contemplated to let go of seeking her mother's love— but to her agony, Genevieve was all she had as a family.

***

"Meet your baby sister, Jodie. Say 'hi' to your sister Penny," Beverly leaned back slightly, propping herself up on one elbow with legs extended in front of her, and baby Penny rested comfortably on her mother's thighs.

On January 5th, 1960, Penny Hess was born, weighing a few pounds and looking exactly like her father. The big sister hopped onto her mother's bed, screeching in glee. The two-year-old Jodie

Hess created a hand-painted paper card for her little sister. Beverly cradled little Penny, allowing Jodie to peck her forehead.

"Her face so soft, Mama," Jodie caressed Penny's face, chuckling as her sister grabbed hold of her little finger. "Mama, when she wake up?"

"I will let you know when she does, sweetie," the three lay down for the afternoon nap, only to be awakened by Melvin's arrival.

The house with two daughters echoed with their shrieking laughter, reverberating wailings, and clamorous stubbornness of the now-able-to-talk Jodie. The matt-painted walls were now doodled with curlicues and abstractions of the two-years-old. The kitchen would remain a clutter of leftover breakfast, uneaten lunch, and grubby last night's dinner utensils till Beverly had put the two to sleep for an afternoon nap. The lounge's carpet, once soft and clean, now had crumbs, marker stains, and grime stuck to it. The center table, which was moved to the corner to protect the two sisters from getting hurt, now had chipped-out corners of the glass top.

The two sisters shared a room as the Hess couldn't afford a bigger house or the construction of a new room. The daughters' room was a sight to behold: wrinkled bedsheets, pillows tossed on the floor, toys scattered across the room, and clothes bursting out of the singular cupboard. The parents' room, more like Beverly's room only, remained seemingly in a better condition with no scatterings except for the one wall where Jodie used to doodle.

They say a messy house homes a happy family, which was true for the Hess family. While Melvin was often away, Beverly kept herself busy with their daughters, filling the house with laughter and activity and maintaining the cleanliness — which was oftentimes a repetitive task in a house of a hyper-active toddler and demanding infant. She rarely found a moment for herself, always surrounded by the joyful chaos of family life.

There were times when Melvin would be away for months, leaving the mother with two little kids. Beverly, still a teenager, took upon the responsibilities of the household and their daughters' upbringing with no grumbles or grievances.

"You know what you are?" Beverly twirled with Penny in her arms, "You are my whole world!" pinching Penny's cheek, "Yes, you are!" blowing a raspberry on Penny's stomach, "Oh, yes, you are!"

"Mommy, up, up!" Jodie bobbed around till Beverly had carefully positioned Penny on the lounge sofa.

"Now, who are you?" Beverly gathered Jodie in her arms and began spinning at a slightly faster pace.

"You are the love of my life! Oh, yes, you are! Beverly's playful teasing was dominated by Jodie's infectious laughter.

Even though the two daughters kept her sufficiently occupied and exhausted, the absence of her loving husband started growing on her. The house, echoing with Jodie's imaginative doll play, would feel nugatory. She dreaded the nighttimes, the only time she would be alone with her thoughts — and her thoughts weren't the presence she ever wanted.

Soon, Beverly found new interests and a lively circle of friends to spend time with. What started as a weekly gathering quickly became a three-nights-a-week affair, with some 'special' friends even staying over and crashing wherever they could find a spot. The gatherings grew larger, and she got comfortable with her new friends. It seemed like Melvin's chronic absence was finally cured by her newfound friends and regular outings. Penny and Jodie also grew comfortable with Beverly's friends, accompanying their mother to brunches, dinners, and after-parties.

"Who'd thought your mother could make so many friends, right?" Beverly talked to no one in particular as they returned from an early afternoon lunch.

"Did you like my new friend, Jodie?" Beverly positioned Penny on the lounge sofa, carefully adjusting the cushions beside her to avoid her from falling.

"My cheek," Jodie said with a frown, rubbing her left cheek. Jodie never liked people who pinched her round cheeks.

"Oh, he was just trying to introduce himself, Jodie. Penny loved him; she laughed at his tickles," Beverly poured a glass of juice for Jodie and herself.

"Penny cried," Jodie climbed the tall stool near the kitchen counter as Beverly placed the juice glass in front of her.

"Ughh, you complain a lot," Beverly swigged the juice, rinsed the glass, and headed back to her room to change into her comfortable clothes. Entering her own bedroom, she was greeted by the hollow stillness of the space. The undone sheets and a haphazard pile of rejected date-night outfits sprawled across the bed welcomed her like silent witnesses to her gaping loneliness.

Beverly's ventures and outings began to escalate at an unexpected pace, often involving the company of the opposite gender. It was her way of attempting to recapture the love she once cherished and basked in with Melvin—a love that now felt like a distant, bittersweet memory. Each encounter seemed like an attempt to fill the growing void within her, a desperate effort to recreate the spark and passion that had once defined her days. Yet, no matter how many outings she embarked on or how lively her social calendar became, an unshakable emptiness lingered, reminding her that some connections simply cannot be replaced.

***

The absence of her one and only took its toll on Beverly. Melvin's absence instilled a feeling of being unloved in Beverly's mind. His care, his warmth, his love—all that made Beverly, Beverly—were taken from her. They say distance makes the heart grow fonder—for Beverly, the distance only matured feelings of abandonment.

Your lips curve so perfectly when you smile, Melvin would trace her lips as if memorizing and cherishing this quiet beauty. Beverly wiped the deep red lipstick with the back of her hand, erasing the memories of the fleeting joy her night-outs brought.

I am glad Jodie took after your eyes, but it isn't as bright as yours, Melvin rested his head into Beverly's lap while snuggling little Jodie. Beverly stripped off the tights, stumbling over the stiff heels she had worn so gracefully.

Caressing her neck, peeling the sleevelet of her dress and pecking the tip of her shoulders, "You have no idea of the privilege you bestow upon me every time you consent to it," Melvin murmured in his deep voice, sending a shiver down her spine. Cladded in her beneath-wears and hugging herself, Beverly stood in front of the mirror, watching the smeared makeup through twinkling eyes. For Melvin, Beverly might have been just a wife at home. Still, to Beverly, Melvin was her definition of everything. After all, what is anyone or anything without a meaningful definition?

Such recollections became an essential part of her post-night-out routine, a quiet ritual that Beverly thought had her anchored to this family… but was it, and for how long? The more the night-outs and outings, the deeper the doldrums gnawed at her.

If I am okay, the family is okay… and I am okay when I am out with friends, for her, such indulgences kept her mind away from the gaping desolation at home. For her, the absence of Melvin's love and attention was a void that could never be filled, yet she knew that such longing did not warrant the denial of the attention that life, in its own way, offered her.

***

One particular friend, a male, frequented his visits to Beverly and her daughters. One of the idiosyncrasies of his visits was the goodbyes — he would leave as soon as the daughters were home and often steal Beverly's kiss.

"Mommy, Daddy kiss?" Jodie's inquiries were brushed off with a telling-off. "Jodie, you don't speak in adults' matters! I don't want to hear anything about it!"

A couple of months passed, and Beverly's frequent male visitor was no longer the same man. This new one was different. He seemed to have little patience for Penny and Jodie, often avoiding them. Unlike the others, he wasn't content to stay for just an afternoon; he would spend the whole day at the Hess house, lounging around, often in Beverly's company. He seemed to enjoy the informality of the household Beverly had invented. The late-night conversations, often overheard by the two daughters, would extend till dawn.

While his presence was a change, there was something unsettling about the way he carried himself around Beverly— winking, nuzzling, and caressing her even in the sisters' presence.

He didn't bother with the usual pleasantries and formalities, or even try to form a connection with Penny and Jodie. It was clear that, unlike the others who had come and gone, this man was here for a singular reason.

One Saturday evening, Beverly invited her newfound friends for a potluck, and the new guy seemed completely glued to her side, regardless of who was around. His attention never wavered, and he remained fixated on Beverly. Whether the conversation was lively or the music was loud, he stayed close, his presence almost possessive. Beverly's other friends called Jodie to dance with them, but she remained by her little sister's side watching her closely in case she fell over.

"You can go and enjoy with your aunties, Jodie. Penny is asleep. I will put her in her crib in the room. Okay? You go, c'mon," following Beverly into the girls' room was her new, smothering male friend.

A couple of minutes later, the new best friends exited the daughters' room and joined everyone seated in the lounge. Beverly's girl friends sang along to the songs and jived to the beats and rhythms. Watching the elder daughter frolicking to the songs, the new guy and Beverly snuck out to the bedroom. Paying no heed to the multitude of guests outside, the lovers retreated to the isolation of the room, the rustling of the fabric, the only sound punctuating the loud music. Lost in each other's touch and passion, the world around them long forgotten.

"It's the bell!" Jodie spoke to no one in particular and waited for a few instants before the bell rang the second time.

Jodie took a deep breath and walked cautiously to the front door. She asked from inside, screaming her query, "Who?"

"Move back from the door, Jodie," the incredibly familiar voice responded, making Jodie squeal in excitement.

The doorlock clicked open, and standing on the doorstep was her father. She froze for a moment, disbelief washing over her as she mouthed the word 'daddy.'

"Daddy!" Jodie threw herself into Melvin's arms as he showered the little one with kisses. After a long, silent hug, Melvin put her down, looking at his daughter with a mixture of emotion, regret, and astonishment in his eyes. "Jodie... I—" he began, but his words faltered upon hearing the music reverberating from inside his house.

Jodie wiped a tear from her cheek, shaking her head. "Daddy, Mom friend," as she grabbed his finger in her hand and pointed towards the lounge.

Melvin entered his house to a scene of a party, "What's going on here? Where's Mom?"

"Mom friend," Jodie said, shifting her focus to Melvin's wristwatch. She gently tapped its display to make the hands move.

Melvin took off the watch and handed it to Jodie, her curiosity sparking a faint smile. "Where's Mom, Jodie?"

"Mom to bed," her face lit with the excitement of receiving a new toy.

"Where's Penny?" Melvin crouched down, his hands on Jodie's shoulders.

"My room," Jodie fumbled with the strap of the wristwatch, trying to fasten it snugly around her tiny wrist.

"Alright, stay here. I will check on Penny and ask Mom to ask her friends to leave. It's past your bedtime. Okay? You go and play," Jodie sprinted toward her aunties to show off her new toy as Melvin headed towards his bedroom.

"Bevs… Bever…" The stark naked sight of his wife with another man had Melvin gobsmacked. Nailed to the ground, he turned pale and motionless. The unexpected intrusion had shocked the two lovers, who scrambled across the bed in a panic, reaching for the sheets to shield themselves from Melvin's wide-eyed gaze.

Beverly, her breath quickening, looked at Melvin with a mix of fear and guilt. She didn't speak, only met his gaze as the silence between them stretched on, heavy with unspoken words. The lover beside awkwardly adjusted the sheets, his eyes flickering between Melvin and Beverly.

"W-What is this?" Melvin's voice finally broke through the haze, barely a whisper, as if he was afraid the words would impale through the very existence of their married life. Beverly didn't answer right away. She seemed to shrink into herself, her eyes downcast, avoiding his gaze.

The man beside her cleared his throat, awkwardly shifting as though trying to find the right moment to speak. But before he could, Beverly stood, shaking her head as she moved toward Melvin. "Melvin, please… let me explain." But her words, meant to soothe, were waved off with a shift in Melvin's countenance.

"Explain?? You have an explanation for this? You had my daughters under the same roof where you were betraying me…" Melvin grabbed her bare shoulder and jolted her, "…and you can explain this… I am…"

"Please, just listen to me," Beverly quivered. This is not what it looks like. This was just…" Beverly turned toward the guy in bed and motioned him to exit. "This was just… you know, just a… fling. This is nothing serious. Trust me."

"Trust you, Beverly? I did, and you betrayed that trust," Melvin, burning with rage, began pacing the room.

"I don't love him, Melvin. I really don't. I have only loved you, and I still do. I do love…" Beverly's futile attempt at reconciliation was met with a stinging slap across her face.

"LOVE ME!? DO YOU KNOW WHAT LOVE IS!?" Melvin grabbed her by her nape, his voice shrill and tone interspersed with stifled wails, "YOU NEVER DID LOVE ME! YOU LOVED THE ATTENTION I GAVE! YOU LOVED THE IDEA OF ME! IF YOU'D HAVE LOVED ME, YOU WOULDN'T HAVE THROWN YOURSELF AT THAT MAN!"

Melvin shoved Beverly roughly toward the bed, and she collapsed onto it, her body sprawled across the sheets. Stunned by his sudden outburst, she lay there in a daze, her mind racing to process what had just happened. The force of his action left her breathless, her heart pounding as she stared up at the ceiling, unable to move, unable to speak.

"The petitioner mentions the domestic abuse. Does the respondent have anything to say or add?" the judge eyed Melvin's attorney from the top of his glasses.

"Yes, Melvin Hess would like to add something," Melvin's attorney gestured for Melvin to stand on the witness stand.

"Your Honor, from the first proceeding of the case, I have stated over and over again that the grounds for this are completely unjustified. I caught Beverly cheating with another man, all while her friends were partying outside in the living room, and my daughters were left on their own — and all that was happening in the same house I bought for her," Melvin heaved a sigh, tightening his grip on the microphone of the witness stand.

"Your Honor, this should have been a case of betrayal and broken trust. My client, Mr. Melvin Hess, has provided sufficient evidence of Mrs. Hess's infidelity. It wasn't the abuse but the affair that caused significant emotional distress and irreparably damaged the marriage," Melvin's attorney provided his reckonings.

"Yes, I admit that I did hit Beverly, but once — ONLY ONE TIME! And that was when I found her in my bed with someone… how else was I supposed to react to finding my wife unclothed with someone else?" in rage, Melvin's voice raised a few decibels, only to be corrected by the smack of a judge's gavel.

"I find this case absolutely groundless, given Mrs. Hess's own 'friends' have testified to her shenanigans. We do understand that Mr. and Mrs. Hess both married young, but that doesn't make disloyalty an excuse … as the petitioners have mentioned previously. We also understand that at such a young age, having uncontrolled desires might be normal, but then again, that doesn't permit infidelity. I rest my case, Your Honor," Melvin's attorney took his seat.

"Does the petitioner want to add or counter the respondent's arguments?" the judge spoke monotonously.

Beverly's attorney rose to his feet, "No, Your Honor."

"The court's decision will consider not only the pieces of evidence of infidelity, but also consider the admission of Mr. Hess to domestic abuse. After careful review of the evidence and testimony presented, this court has reached a decision." The judge adjusted his glasses, glancing between Beverly and Melvin. "while the petitioner has made serious allegations against the respondent, the evidence does not conclusively establish grounds for a fault-based divorce. Therefore, the charges of domestic abuse are dismissed."

Melvin leaned back, gulping down a glass of water while Beverly had her face buried in her hands. The judge continued, "This court will proceed with the divorce on no-fault grounds, citing irreconcilable differences. Both parties are strongly encouraged to work towards a certain settlement to avoid further emotional and marital strain."

The gavel was struck for the last time: "The court is adjourned."

As the courtroom emptied, Beverly sat there motionless, her mind reeling. The charges were dropped, and now she had to return to the same house. It felt as if justice had slipped through her fingers. Melvin exited the room without a single glance in her direction, with his attorney close behind.

Beverly and Melvin arrived home in the same cab in complete silence — no arguments, no exchange of expletives, no foul speech. Their eyes were glued to the cab window to the rather contrastingly lively scenery outside. The two daughters, who fell asleep on the courtroom benches, now napped on the shoulder and lap of their mother. The cab came to a screeching halt right outside their *house* while the couple remained seated, unsure of how to proceed after all the court proceedings.

"Sir, are we at the right house?" the cab driver turned around to ask Melvin.

"Apologies. Yes, we are at the right house," Melvin got out of the car, opened the door for Beverly, and warily took the sleeping Jodie in his arms, ensuring she remained asleep.

The click of the lock followed by the footfall remained the only resonances to be sounded in the Hess household for that remaining day. Beverly had locked herself up in her bedroom with both Penny and Jodie. Melvin lounged around the living room and their daughter's room, his presence a mere lingering. As the nighttime approached, Melvin pan-heated the leftovers and plated some for Beverly and the daughters.

Sniffling and brushing away the stray tears, Melvin knocked on his bedroom door, "Beverly, Jodie must be hungry by now. I have reheated some leftovers for her … and you," Melvin's inquiry was met by a sighing silence, "I won't come inside. I will just sleep in Jodie's room. I am leaving the plate right outside the door. Take it."

As Melvin dragged the chair off the dining table, the bedroom door clicked open and thudded close. Jodie's bed was too small for Melvin to fit in, so he decided to lay down the mattress on the floor and sleep there. Beverly had put to sleep her two daughters, Jodie's faint snores piercing the heavy silence.

Did I actually make her feel so unloved...Was she ever loyal to me? Was I never enough? If yes, then what is this... Melvin stared blankly into the darkness of the room, vision clouded by the tears threatening to make him bawl.

Did I never love him enough...Will he ever love me the same way? Will I ever have his trust? If not, then why keep on with this... Beverly rubbed the crown of Penny's head and cuddled her close, sobbing her eyes out as her body shook with quiet grief.

I loved you with all my heart... oh, how much I have missed you, the unspoken, unconsoled sorrow finally broke down Melvin's resistance. *I longed for you, Melvin, I still do... even now...* Beverly covered her mouth with both hands to stifle the cry, her heart breaking at the thought of everything that had slipped away.

In the midst of their individual sorrows and melancholia, there was an undeniable truth: the love they once had, the trust they nurtured was still there — fractured and strained.

Chapter 4: Missing Pieces

"Let's make you breakfast. Jodie, wake up," Beverly ran her fingers through Jodie's hair, tucking the stray strands behind her ear.

Beverly, cradling Penny, exited the bedroom tiptoeing her way toward the kitchen to not wake up the now-estranged husband. Jodie went on to catch her forty winks on the couch before breakfast was prepared. Beverly settled down little Penny beside Jodie and quietly arranged the breakfast. She even kept the flame on medium so as to avoid the sizzle of oil in a hot pan.

"C'mon, breakfast is ready. It is scrambled eggs," Beverly helped Jodie up, handing her a glass of hot milk to wake her up.

Beverly only had a glass of some fresh juice and a piece of sausage as she helped Jodie gulp down her scrambled eggs. Almost noiselessly, Beverly washed the dishes, cleaned the kitchen, and went on to check on Penny sleeping in the lounge when the slightly ajar door of her daughters' room caught her sight.

"Jodie, go check if someone is inside," Beverly lifted Penny from her resting position as she gestured at Jodie.

Jodie pushed the door completely open, revealing an empty room shrouded in darkness. "No, Mama," Jodie darted back to her mother, seeing her room in complete darkness for the first time.

"Come on, let's see where your father went," Beverly ruffled Jodie's hair.

Beverly turned on the lights, bringing to notice a well-made bed and signs of abandonment. *What if he is hiding from me?* She crouched down to look under the bed only to expose the absurdity of her thought. She knocked on the bathroom door thrice before turning the lock to open, hoping to barge in on her soon-to-be-divorced husband. *Where can he be? What if he went out to have breakfast?* Beverly strutted towards the house entrance, expecting to find his faux leather sandals out of place. The leather brown sandal was still in its place, with no indication of being taken out of the rack.

"Wait a second, where did he go?" Beverly, positioning Penny on the couch, walked outside her house to see if her husband was turning the corner.

"Jodie, go and ask at your friend's house if your dad is there," Beverly quickly strapped Jodie's sandals and watched her from the threshold. Jodie returned with a 'no' — an answer she anticipated but didn't want to hear.

"He must have left a note somewhere," Beverly searched the dining table, the bedside table in her daughters' room, and the lounge table, burying her face in her hands in frustration.

"Mommy, no cry, no cry," Jodie placed her head into Beverly's lap, attempting to comfort her.

"How can he just get up and leave? What am I to do now? I thought I could talk it out," Beverly let out a shuddering sob, "How can he think this is over? After all that I have been through because of him..." Beverly embraced Jodie, "I did everything for you girls. I did everything for him, and he thinks this is all over."

Jodie started sobbing, watching her mother in such agony as she freed herself from Beverly's embrace and wiped her mother's tears, "No cry, no cry..."

Beverly rubbed her face dry, fixed Jodie's disheveled hair, and finger-combed them, "You are right, you are right. I don't have to cry. If he left, he did it on his own. I had no problem with him living here. But what do I do?"

"Here, Jodie, you do your coloring, and I will check on Penny," Beverly had Jodie seated on the couch and handed her a notebook and pencil colors to keep her distracted from her breakdown.

Pacing the room in silence punctuated by Penny's cooing and sighing, Beverly had her mouth covered with a hand to stifle her sobs. *Am I a bad woman that I don't even deserve a chance to explain,* snuffling, Beverly began biting her nails and cuticles. *I am the mother of his daughters.... He can't simply leave and forget about that,* Beverly rubbed her neck, her fingers trembling as if trying to claw away the invisible weight pressing against her throat, squeezing the air from her lungs. *How do I tell him I have loved only him... there never can be anyone else... Oh, Melvin,* Beverly pulled at her hair as cold sweat broke out on her skin. The voices inside her head overwhelmed her, blurring her vision and muffling the voices around.

"Mama, I drew a bird! Look, look—a bird!" Jodie exclaimed, waving her colored drawing in the air. Beverly, slipping further from reality, tried to steady herself. Her arms flailing as she reached for the wall. But collapsed to the floor before she could touch it. "Mama! Mama!" Jodie rushed towards her mother, cupping her mother's face in her tiny hands, "You good?"

"I am fine, I am fine. Don't worry. It was just Mommy fell asleep standing," Beverly gathered Jodie in her arms, "That's such a beautiful bird, Jodie," she took the paper from her daughter's hands, "We will hang it on the kitchen wall, okay? Good work!" Beverly pecked the top of Jodie's head and checked on little Penny, who remained unbothered and deep asleep.

"Let's first call your grandmother, okay? Because I don't know who else to call. She is all I have now," Jodie held onto her mother's hand as they made their way towards the telephone holder.

Beverly dialed her mother's number twice and received no response. At the third attempt, her stepfather picked up the phone, who refused to recognize her voice and almost immediately disconnected the call. Beverly dialed the fourth time, and this time, it was her mother who picked up.

"Mother, this is Beverly," Beverly spoke in a softer tone.

"Well, I never expected this, but why did you call?" Genevieve remained cold in her tones, each word sharp and unyielding.

"I apologize if my call had disturbed you, but I have no one left to call after... Melvin," the quiver in Beverly's tone spoke volumes about her reason to call.

"What do you mean? He died or something?" a possible tragedy spoken with a rather plain nonchalance.

"No, no, not that. He left me and the girls," Beverly tightened her grip on the receiver as if quelling the sob threatening to break her down.

"Oh, that's very much like the laggard he was," Genevieve rolled her eyes and smacked her lips, "Did he transfer the house to you?"

"I don't know. I am alone here with my daughters. We never talked about this. He was mostly away for work, and I was left here to look after the girls and the house," Jodie had now clung to her mother's legs, drenching her colored drawing with her tears.

"That's is beyond maddening, Beverly. You should come here," Chris said to his wife, and Genevieve shushed him away with a wave of her hand.

"Can I? I don't have to stay here anymore... not without Melvin," Beverly gently patted Jodie's head in consolation.

"I will have Chris send you a money wire of $55, and you can come here with your girls," Genevieve blew the filing residue.

"Thank you, mother. I owe you. I'll let you know when I receive the money wire, and then I will be on my way. Bye now," Beverly lifted Jodie up in her arms and peppered her with kisses.

"We're going to grandma! We're going to grandma!" Beverly tossed her up only to catch a hysterically laughing Jodie.

Beverly left for Nebraska a few days after receiving the money wire of $55. The train journey to Lincoln was a blur of stifled sobs, forced smiles to keep her daughters entertained, and sleepless nights that bled into weary days. The train screeched to a halt on the Lincoln station. There, Genevieve sat waiting for her daughter and grandchildren with a smile that never seemed to reach her eyes. Genevieve stepped forward, arms outstretched, and she quickly gave the guests a half-hearted embrace.

"Finally, you are here. Get your baggage, and let's get you settled," Genevieve strutted out of the station with a half-smoked cigarette dangling between two of her fingers.

"Mother, what about..." Beverly shouldered three of her bags while dragging the bigger suitcases.

"Nah-ahh, not now. First, get home, and then we can talk. Not here," Genevieve took her seat in the car, ignoring the fact that

Beverly would have to squeeze onto a single seat with her two daughters and their luggage.

Beverly, with two bags stacked on her lap, exhaled in relief. She kept glancing at little Penny in her arms, making sure she remained asleep. Jodie, wide-eyed, gaped at the buildings and scenery of Lincoln, completely mesmerized. With nothing but painful memories left in Carolina, Beverly had risked everything on Genevieve's promise of a fresh start.

The streets of Lincoln were familiar to Beverly, yet she found herself strangely disoriented. They drove past rows of apartment buildings, but something weighed down Beverly's aspirations to start anew in Lincoln. *Soon, I will have a home for my girls, a space of our own,* Beverly forced a weak smile, lifting Penny up to rest on her shoulder.

The car swerved sharply into the driveway of the Miller house, coming to an abrupt stop. The sudden brake sent Jodie lurching forward while Beverly jolted against the bags resting on her lap. "Careful, mister! Watch where you are going," Genevieve pushed the door open and trotted towards the Miller house.

"But, Mother, I thought we were going to…" Beverly struggled to unlock the trunk of the car with Penny resting on one shoulder.

"I told you, Beverly, not outside. We'll talk inside," Genevieve's smile tightened.

"But, I thought you found an apartment," Beverly spoke under her breath as she took the suitcases out of the car's trunk.

She followed Genevieve inside, clutching Jodie's hands as they stepped over the threshold. The house smelled of polished wood and freshly brewed coffee, a stark contrast to the uncertainty gnawing at

Beverly's gut. She set their bags down, shifting her weight uncomfortably.

"Come inside," Genevieve patted the seat beside her, "Sit here."

Beverly obeyed unhesitatingly, but a familiar unease gnawed at her, "What is it, Mother? I thought we would stay in a separate apartment. Why did you bring us here?"

"Do you want something to drink? It must have been a long journey," Genevieve said, getting up and taking Penny from Beverly's embrace. Here, let me put her to sleep. You can rest a while."

Chris came with a couple of glasses filled with freshly squeezed fruit juices, "Take her with you. Show her the toys Grandma bought for her. Go on," Genevieve gestured to Chris, who handed Jodie a glass of juice and took her inside.

"Beverly," Genevieve began, rocking Penny back and forth, "you know, the girls are little, and they need stability. I don't think it is good for them to go on an apartment search with you."

Beverly's stomach dropped. "What? Mother, what are you saying?"

Genevieve sighed, her expression almost pitying. "The girls can stay here. But you... you can't."

For a moment, the words didn't register. "But you said—"

"I said I'd help, and I have. This is what's best for them." Genevieve's voice was firm, final.

Beverly shot to her feet, snatching Penny from her mother's arms, "No! You promised me a place. You can't just—"

85

Genevieve leaped to her feet, almost intimidating her. "And where would you go? You don't have a place to live. You don't have a job. You don't have any way to provide for them. Do you want them to suffer?"

Tears welled up in Beverly's eyes. The reality was exposed in all its ugliness. The moment she decided to leave Melvin's house, she knew for a fact her past might come hunting her down. Melvin wasn't just her partner or a father to her daughters, but a barrier she strongly relied on to keep her past firmly at bay. *What else did I expect from the woman who ruined my childhood?* Beverly glanced at her mother, sipping her fresh juice, fully aware that once again, she would have Beverly and her daughters firmly under her control.

The room seemed to close in around her, the walls pressing against her chest. She looked at Penny, her innocent eyes twinkling with joy upon seeing her mother, and she knew. She had no power here. No way to fight back.

Genevieve reached for Penny, and Beverly dejectedly handed her her little girl. Beverly found herself unraveling. "Please," she whispered. "Don't do this."

However, Genevieve already had thought of it — for her, it was all according to her plan.

She had laid the groundwork, woven the manipulation. The apartment that never existed. The whispered accusations that would come later—that Beverly had abandoned them and left them alone in a filthy room with no food, no water, no hope. A lie strong enough to bury the truth.

Beverly stumbled toward the door, every instinct screaming at her to fight, but there was nothing left to fight with — no justification would ever undo what Genevieve had already planned. Genevieve had won.

And she never saw it coming…and the worst was yet to come.

***

A couple of weeks went by, and the only place Beverly could find for her and her daughters was a tiny apartment situated in the commercial area. The peeling wall, the largely stained floor, and the constant dripping of the water awaited Beverly's homecoming. The kitchen was merged into the living room, leaving no space for furniture to be adjusted. The bedroom was a couple-feet distance from the living room with a tiny attached bathroom — that was the only washing and bathing area in the entire house. The ceiling was blistered with paint bubbles, bursting to flake. The large window in the living room remained the singular way to ventilate the house.

The loosely nailed lock rattled and scraped as Beverly tried to unbolt it. A few more jolts later, the door unlocked, leaving Beverly with the unfastened lock and key in her hand. Creaking it open, Beverly pushed her suitcase inside and flicked the light switch, illuminating the life she ended up having. A sour, moldy smell clung to the walls, followed by a ricocheting drip. Beverly did a quick, minute-long tour of her new house, unpacked the new cleaning tools, and began scrubbing, mopping, and sweeping her new dwelling.

Home was with Melvin, with my daughters… home is probably what I will never find or have… pulling in quick breath through her nose, Beverly steadied herself while mopping. The earthy scent of mildew seemed like to have enduring residence in this place. Though cleaned and dust-free, homeliness remained amiss.

In a days' time, Beverly found a wage-based job in a restaurant working as a server. The emoluments were sufficient to keep the kids fed and the house running. Despite the long hours, Beverly made sure the girls were always in safe care. At times, Genevieve would visit the two girls during the afternoon to ensure their well-being.

One day, Genevieve and Christian went to Beverly's apartment to check on how their grandkids were. From behind the closed door, Genevieve heard the foreign voices: manly and deeper in resonance. The usual knocking turned into a raged door-banging followed by screaming imprecations.

"I knew it! Beverly, how could you..." Genevieve turned her gaze towards the little girls, "with the kids here!"

The man, dressed in overalls, emerged from the bedroom. "With Him!?" Genevieve crouched down and embraced the obviously shocked Jodie and the now-crying Penny.

"No, no, no! It's not like that! Whatever you are thinking, you are wrong, Mother!" Beverly motioned to the man to wait outside and to exit the house, and he did as told.

"There's no way I will allow you to keep the kids with you!" Genevieve roughly snatched the crying Penny from the couch, wrenched open the cupboard in the bedroom, and stuffed the kids' clothes in a bag.

Beverly seized her mother by the shoulders, forcing her to face her, and reached out to take Penny from her arms. Her efforts to stop her mother were swiftly met with a sharp slap across the face.

"You will not question my authority here, Beverly. You have been a disgrace to me and our family... and I won't let you disgrace these little girls as well," Genevieve shoved Beverly towards bed, "Let's go, Chris. I won't stay here for another minute," she dragged Jodie out of the house, whose insistent cries were quietened by a loud reprimand.

Chasing her mother's cab down the road, running barefooted, and screaming her implorations, Beverly was robbed of her right to be a mother to her children in a moment's notice. She returned home to a void, a silence more unbearable than the creaking of the floorboards or the dripping faucet. The absence of Jodie and Penny carved a deep ache within her chest, making the musty walls close in around her. She paced the small apartment, every corner screaming of their presence now gone. The air, thick with mildew and grief, clung to her skin.

Days passed, each one stretching endlessly as Beverly sought answers. She knocked on doors, made calls, and demanded explanations, but none came. Whether out of malice or misplaced righteousness, Genevieve and Chris had taken her children, and no one seemed willing to help her get them back. The legal void surrounding the situation left Beverly in a tormenting limbo—her daughters had been taken, and yet, there was no record, no official ruling, no avenue for her to reclaim them. She changed jobs, switched from one workplace to another, and worked day and night to have sufficient money to claim her kids back.

***

...Melvin's distress

Melvin creased the envelope and stamped the wax seal, smudging the receiving address inked on the front. Overwriting the smudged letters, Melvin ran a hand over his face, exhaling in exhaustion. This was one of the many letters Melvin had sent Genvieve, wishing to hear more about his daughters. He had done everything he could think of—every month, another letter sent to Mrs. Genevieve, pleading, demanding, bargaining. Anything to bring his daughters back to him. But his queries remained unanswered.

The first of those many letters was sent from Kannapolis, Ohio. Inquiring about his daughters' well-being, it was accompanied by $20, a mix of coins, and multiple crumpled bills.

By October, he had been working steadily at the Air Force base in Fairborn, Ohio, even making sure the girls had insurance. Surely that counted for something? He'd written again, reminding Genevieve of his stability, of his commitment. His anticipation to acquire custody was assuaged by embellished reassurances...

November had been the hardest. The uncertainty gnawed, and the unresponsiveness built on his desperation. He had written again, almost groveling, asking if his daughters were even still there. He had considered calling Mrs. Skinner himself, but he hesitated, fearing the same silence would greet him on the other end of the line. Even though he knew he was talking to a woman who had already decided he wasn't a good father, Melvin continued writing to her.

Then came December. He had heard whispers of a hearing in January, a chance to make his case. But would she even show up? Would he be given a chance to fight for his daughters' custody? Or should he simply accept this as fate?

January arrived, and the new year brought nothing but more hopelessness. He still had no work. He wished he could have his girls with him, wished more than anything that he could be the father they needed. But how could he bring them back into a life where he couldn't even put food on the table? The father he dreamt to be seemed like a distant thought…

Genevieve took the last letter she received from Melvin and placed it atop the rest of his letters, stuffing them into a black bag, ready to be tossed into the trash.

***

Little Penny was just two months shy of her first birthday when a swelling on her leg demanded urgent medical attention. At first, it appeared as nothing more than a small bump—an irritation easily dismissed. But as days passed, the redness deepened, the swelling grew, and Penny's fussiness turned into inconsolable cries of pain. Genevieve, who had been watching over her grandkids at the time, noticed the change but chose to keep it to herself.

Rather than informing Beverly, she convinced herself that it was something minor, something that could be managed without causing unnecessary panic. Perhaps it was stubborn pride, or maybe something more calculated—an opportunity to strengthen her own hold over the child. So, she waited. She dabbed at the wound with homemade remedies and whispered reassurances to herself that it would heal in time. But it didn't.

By the time the infection could no longer be ignored, Penny's grandmother finally decided to call Beverly, especially since Penny was still under Melvin's military medical insurance, nullifying her forced guardianship.

"What happened to my baby?" Beverly asked, taking her groaning baby in her arms. " Shush, shush, Mama is here. It's all right." Beverly tried rocking her to sleep, but the discomfort seemed to outdo the motherly love Penny hadn't had in a long while.

"Don't ask me what happened! It's all your doing. If you weren't busy with other men, your daughter wouldn't have been in this state," Genevieve hurled the baby bag towards Beverly, causing Penny's essentials and clothes to scatter on the living room floor.

"But, Mother, you used to visit them at my place, and…" a pinch on Beverly's arm interrupted her justification, making her squeal in agony.

"Don't try to put this on me, you good-for-nothing mother! If I were to cause them pain, you wouldn't know about it at all… Now get this sick daughter of yours out of my place before she makes us all sick!" Genevive released her grip, shunting Beverly.

"Can I see Jodie before I leave?" Genevieve grabbed a handful of Beverly's upper arm, dragged her towards the house entrance, and shoved her out, slamming the door shut on her face.

When the doctors diagnosed it as an abscess requiring immediate intervention, she sat alone in the hospital, signing the consent forms with a shaky hand. The procedure was swiftly carried out, draining the infection and saving Penny from further harm, but it left a small, permanent scar on her delicate skin—a mark of both healing and secrecy.

Days later, when Penny's leg seemed to be healing and improving, a multitude of knocks on Beverly's apartment jolted her awake from her much-needed slumber. Genevieve made way to Beverly's bedroom, clasping her granddaughter to her bosom.

"I will take her home to her sister. You can't be trusted again with the care of your own children," Genevieve put a pacifier into Penny's mouth to assuage her relentless sobs.

"She is still recovering from her surgery. I can't let you steal my daughter from me!" Beverly's protestations were met with Genevieve's vociferous vilification.

Once again, Beverly's motherhood was questioned … once again, a mother's love was twisted by cruelty. This time, there was no calling after her mother, no running barefooted on the street, and no screaming… this time, it was acceptance, silent yet resounding.

Dimissive towards Beverly's attitude, laced with condescension, Genevieve spoke her parting words, "I will take it from here. It's better this way."

But Penny's mother knew better. This wasn't care—it was control. And that tiny scar became more than just a mark left behind by a medical procedure. It became a tool of manipulation, a reminder of Genevieve's unspoken message: *I know what's best. I decide what matters. You were never needed.*

"There is some mail addressed to you, Genevieve," Christian browsed through the stack of envelopes before setting them in front of Genevieve, who was fixing her cigar.

"Can you read me who is it from?" Genevieve filled the cigar with the fermented leaves, paying no heed to the letter scattered on the center table.

"One is from Melvin's mother, Mrs. Hess…" Christian furrowed his brows, "is it something about Beverly?"

"Leave that one on the table; don't open it," Genevieve put down the cigar and tore open the letter.

The letter was a response to Genevieve's own, manipulating Beverly's misconduct and justifying her swift decision to bring the children into her care. Grandma Hess expressed her appreciation for

Genevieve's supposed consideration, writing of her disbelief at Beverly's behavior and how unfortunate it was that the children had to suffer the consequences of their mother's actions.

For Genevieve, letter writing became more than just a means of communication—it was a tool of control, a way to shape the narrative to her advantage. Through carefully chosen words, she painted herself as the only one truly concerned and capable guardian of Penny and Jodie while simultaneously casting doubt on Beverly's ability to be a responsible mother. With each letter, she reinforced the image of a selfless grandmother stepping in to protect her innocent grandchildren from neglect and instability.

Most of these letters were addressed to Melvin Hess, Grandma Hess, and occasionally to Beverly. To Melvin and Grandma Hess, Genevieve emphasized her unwavering devotion, highlighting the sacrifices she made for the children's well-being. Grandma Hess was mostly worried about the children's welfare, being insistent on allowing her to speak to Beverly and her children. Her letters entailed greetings and prayers for her granddaughters and Beverly, with subtle insertion of updates on Melvin's work.

When writing to Beverly, however, her tone was different. It was less about her own role and more about reinforcing Beverly's shortcomings. She seldom offered words of encouragement, instead subtly reminding her daughter of past failures and suggesting that any hope of regaining custody depended entirely on Genevieve's approval.

Beverly's letters informed Genevieve of her accident, starvation, and failure to find any work in Little Rock, but Genevieve remained cold towards her own daughter. The following month, in another letter, Beverly updated her mother about her life and change in address to Bobby Orr's house, hoping a change in location would lead to a fresh start. She wrote to her girls, sending love through words she could only hope reached them: "Mommy loves you very, very much. More than Grandma will ever love Mommy. Don't let anyone be mean to her girls."

Beverly found a job in a Memphis factory, the first flicker of hope in several days. She firmly believed she could finally bring her daughters home. But another obstacle arose when she moved to Chicago that same month, facing surgery and reaching out once more, asking for pictures of her daughters.

To showcase her stability and sense of responsibility, Beverly sent money. However, soon enough, the bitter truth settled in. She had been sending money, but Genevieve wasn't interested in reuniting her with her children. Instead, she encouraged her to chase Melvin for child support while rerouting her payments directly to Genevieve. Genevieve had told her about the child safety worker, Mrs. Skinner, in one of her response letters, so Beverly decided to contact this safety worker. When she called Mrs. Skinner, hoping to find out what more she had to do, all she got in return was a cold dismissal without any apparent reason. No explanation.

An investigator in Chicago reviewed her case and saw no reason why she shouldn't have her children. But words on a report meant nothing against the silent, unyielding walls built by those who had already decided she was unfit.

She had a new address now, another fresh start. But no matter how many times she moved, how much she sent, or how desperately she reached out, she remained on the outside looking in.

As time passed, Beverly and Melvin's interactions with Penny and Jodie became filtered through Genevieve's letters. They were no longer direct participants in their daughters' lives but mere spectators, dependent on whatever version of events Genevieve chose to share. Phone calls were rare, visits even rarer, and the only updates they received came in the form of letters filled with Genevieve's interpretations of the children's lives.

Each letter to Melvin and Beverly was laced with carefully placed reassurances, offering the false hope that one day, when either of them proved stable enough, the children would be returned. But that day never seemed to come. Instead, Genevieve continued to solidify her position as Penny and Jodie's rightful guardian, ensuring that with every passing letter, her hold over them—and over the truth—grew even stronger.

Genevieve's lies climaxed when, one afternoon, her home phone rang. Upon greeting the caller, Genevieve found herself short on words to carry with her lies, "How is everything, Mrs. Hess? How is your husband?"

"We are fine and healthy. How are you and your husband… and my granddaughters'?" Grandma Hess asked hesitantly.

"Oh, they are absolutely wonderful! The two keep me busy all day," Genevieve feigned a laugh.

"Oh, they must, especially Penny, since she is so little," Grandma Hess attempted to keep the conversation going.

"Yes. A few days back, she fell sick also, so I had to tend to her tantrums and medications… and, of course, the sleepless nights…" Genevieve's self-praise was cut short.

"Any chance I can speak to them?" Grandma Hess sat with her fingers crossed, hoping to hear her granddaughter's voice the next minute.

"Oh, Mrs. Hess. I am so sorry. I could have put Jodie on the phone, but they aren't here. You see, Beverly came the other day, grabbed my granddaughters by their hands, and dragged them out. I mean, she didn't even tell me where she took them. I have been worried about them ever since…" Genevieve sniffled, pretending to be emotional.

"Oh goodness! What is wrong with Beverly? She has never been like this. Were Penny and Jodie okay when she left with them?" Grandma Hess was bewildered by this revelation as Genevieve continued weaving and ingraining her lies.

"Mrs. Hess, you must know, even the child safety worker, Mrs. Skinner, never approved of this behavior from Beverly. Mrs. Skinner clearly instructed me to keep them away from Beverly as she could, in one way or the other, harm the kids. You do understand the stress I am in right now, right, Mrs. Hess?" Genevieve let out a theatrical wail.

Grandma Hess gasped, her voice trembling with concern. "Oh dear, Genevieve, I—I had no idea things had gotten this bad. Poor Penny and Jodie. Are you sure Beverly didn't say anything at all before taking them?"

Genevieve seized the moment, lowering her voice to a sorrowful whisper. "Mrs. Hess, I wish I didn't have to say this, but you must face the truth. Beverly isn't the woman she once was. She has changed. The stress, the bad influences… I fear she's completely lost her way. And now, she's dragged the girls into this mess with her."

There was a long pause on the other end of the line before Grandma Hess finally spoke. "I'll talk to Melvin about this. Maybe we should reach out to Mrs. Skinner, too."

Genevieve tightened her grip on the receiver, her lips curling into a triumphant smile before quickly schooling her expression back into one of worry. "Yes, yes, that would be wise. I just pray it's not too late."

But Beverly did not know that Mrs. Skinner was never a real caseworker or someone positioned to help. She was likely a friend of Genevieve's who used to foul play the part of a social worker and add legitimacy to Genevieve's manipulation of both Beverly and Melvin.

"Melvin has been worried sick about his daughters, but them being with Beverly somehow assuaged his worries. Goodness me, how will I tell him all this? He has been trying so hard to find a stable job, but employment isn't easy to find these days. You do understand, Mrs. Miller?" Grandma Hess swallowed hard, awaiting another biting jeer.

"Yes, of course, you already told me, which is why I still think that the kids should stay with me till both their parents are stable enough — both mentally and financially — to responsibly take care of them," Genevieve smiled to her slyly, coiling a strand of hair around her finger. "Alright, Mrs. Hess, I have some commitments to attend to. Hope to speak soon. Have a good day."

That was the last time Grandma Hess spoke to Genevieve, fully aware of Genevieve's intent to never hand the kids over to either of the parents. Penny's wailing stirred the prevailing silence right on the dead tone of the phone. *Guess, I have another helper to raise and train,* Genevieve scolded Jodie out of the room for disturbing her sister's slumber and rocked little Penny back to sleep. The reprimands were directed more towards a few-years-old Jodie, who was mostly told to stay away from her sister.

Regardless of the reason behind Penny's crying, Jodie would receive an earful about being a mean and bad sister. Throughout Penny's crawling days, it was always Jodie who bore the blame whenever her baby sister got so much as a bruise. Genevieve had strict instructions to maintain the tranquility of the house. If Penny's cries lingered too long, Genevieve wouldn't hesitate to shut her in a room, just to "restore order." Penny's sobs would be muffled behind the door, and no one dared challenge it.

As for Jodie, she was moved into her own room under the guise of growing up. Genevieve called it *training*. To her, it was to teach her to sleep alone, to be brave, to conquer her fear of the dark. But to Jodie, it felt more like exile. Her small bed sat beneath a drafty window, the shadows in the corners growing longer each night. She'd lie stiff under the covers, wide-eyed, listening to the creaks and murmurs of the house, and the occasional cry of Penny behind her own closed door. Some nights, Jodie whispered to herself to stay strong. Other nights, she called out for her mother, whispering apologies into the dark for things she didn't do and couldn't stop. For her tiny mind, the separation from her mother was a punishment bestowed because of her poor behavior, oblivious to the viciousness of her grandma's manipulation.

One afternoon, when Penny was settled down for her nap, Jodie decided to ask the pressing question, "Grandma, where is mama?" This question became the kernel of Genevieve's lifelong manipulation.

"Sweetheart, wherever your mom is, she is not with you… and you are safe here away from your mom," Genevieve plucked her up and have her sit on the couch.

"I want mama," Jodie pouted, observing the quiet triumph in her Grandma's eyes as her lips faintly lifted into a suggestion of a smile.

"But mama doesn't want you, my child," Genevieve ran her hand through Jodie's hair, eyebrows arched in amusement, almost confident of the game she had begun.

"Mama loves me, Grandma… she says it," Jodie's voice trembled, her chin quivering.

"Oh no, my child, no crying," Genevieve dabbed Jodie's face, "Your mother is not a good girl like you. You are my little angel, and you don't need to cry when you have me, right?" Genevieve embraced her, pecking her forehead. It was the kind of expression that could be mistaken for warmth. The trouble is Genevieve's warmth is as pernicious as any perceived danger. That embrace — deliberate and measured — was an emotional engineering guised as a consolation.

"I am your guardian now, Jodie," Genevieve said, gently placing Jodie's head on the shoulder pad of the blazer. Your grandma will take very good care of you and Penny. You just have to listen to your grandma, okay, sweetheart?" Genevieve patted her back, attempting to soothe Jodie's hiccupping cries.

Beverly sniffled and quickly dried her eyes, her train of thought was cruelly interrupted by a bus whooshing by, almost making her lose the divorce notice she received. She blinked hard, fighting the sting in her eyes, refusing to let them well up again. She couldn't afford to cry again. Not tonight. Not after leaving her girls in Genevieve's house—a place that wore warmth like a mask but never truly welcomed it.

She thought of Jodie, of Penny, of how small they'd looked watching her walk away. How Jodie will have to be brave for herself and her little sister, fearing how her innocence and childhood will be brutally taken away from her.

"I'm doing this for them," she whispered to herself, pressing her lips together. "Just until I get on my feet."

She heaved a sigh, squared her shoulders, and crossed the street toward a dingy café with a help wanted sign half-taped to the door. One more try. One more shot to claw her way back to her daughters.

* * *

Beverly entered a new relationship with a man named Bobby Orr, eventually changing her address to match his. The relationship grew not out of romance at first, but out of Beverly's deep longing to reunite with her daughters.

Bobby offered steady reassurance and unwavering presence, which Beverly hadn't felt in a long time. Though slightly older than Beverly, Bobby was drawn to her strength and vulnerability, and he found her deeply attractive even after learning the full extent of her difficult circumstances. For Beverly, his consistency became a lifeline during an uncertain and emotionally charged chapter of her life.

The early days of Beverly and Bobby's relationship were shaped by a shared mission: finding a way to reunite Beverly with her daughters. Each day brought new challenges, and most nights ended the same: Beverly crying herself to sleep in Bobby's arms, clinging to hope while unaware of the quiet depth of his growing feelings.

For Bobby, what began as support soon evolved into something more. But the weight of Beverly's pain, and the uncertainty of where he stood in her heart, became too much to ignore. One fateful day, as Beverly broke down in anguish once again, Bobby found himself at a crossroads as he could no longer carry the emotional burden in

101

silence. He knew he had to either step fully into this relationship or gently step away before either of them broke further.

The first time Beverly stepped into Bobby Orr's apartment, she wasn't thinking about romance, but refuge. She clutched the handle of her suitcase with white-knuckled fingers, her eyes darting nervously around the modest living room. He met her at the door, gently taking the bag from her hand.

"It's not much," Bobby said, giving a sheepish glance around the space. "But you're safe here."

That night, Beverly barely spoke. She stared out the window for hours, her thoughts lost in memories of her daughters. Bobby made tea and left it untouched on the table beside her. He didn't press her. He just sat nearby, quiet, like a steady shadow.

In those early days, their bond formed not through words but through silence. Through the shared meals, she barely touched. Through the careful way he always kept the couch cushions fluffed, the towels warm from the dryer. And when the tears came—as they always did—he never said "don't cry." He just held her, letting her grief spill out into the dark.

They ate together on the couch, cross-legged, sharing bites and laughing over absolutely nothing. They would go on strolls, walking hand-in-hand, simply enjoying each other's presence and company. For a few moments, it felt like the world outside had paused while some days stretched to endless worry and anxiety.

Weeks passed. The apartment began to feel less like a shelter and more like a waiting room for a life that hadn't yet returned. Beverly was still without her daughters. Bobby was still by her side. But now, little things started to surface.

"You left the porch light on again," Beverly snapped one evening, arms crossed in the doorway.

"I thought you liked it on," Bobby replied, confused.

"Well, I don't!" she shot back, the frustration spilling out faster than she meant.

They stared at each other for a long moment. It wasn't really about the light. It was about the pressure, the helplessness, the unspoken weight pressing down on both of them.

Later that night, Beverly muttered a quiet "sorry" as she folded laundry in the dim light. Bobby walked over and took a shirt from her hands, folding it alongside her.

"We're both trying," he said simply.

And they were.

One morning, Beverly didn't feel like getting out of bed. Her stomach had been unsettled for days, and she couldn't shake the feeling that something had changed.

She stared at the ceiling, then at the calendar.

A slow, trembling realization crept in.

Later that afternoon, she sat across from Bobby at the kitchen table, twisting a spoon in her hands.

"I think I'm pregnant," she said, barely above a whisper.

Bobby blinked. Once. Twice.

Silence settled between them like dust. Then he reached for her hand. "Okay," he said. "We'll figure it out."

She looked up at him, searching his face for judgment, fear, anything. But all she saw was the same quiet steadiness that had been there since day one.

"Bobby," she said, her voice tight, "I don't even know where my life is going right now. I don't know if I can do this."

"You're not doing it alone," he said firmly.

For the first time in a long time, she believed someone when they said that.

Weeks later, the reality weighed her down. She still couldn't figure out a way to bring back her daughters, and the worries of a newborn smothered her. The blur of days blending into uncertainty and uncontrolled sobbing. Bobby stayed steadfast and patient with her, watching the woman he had come to love unravel before him.

"I can't keep going like this," he murmured, voice raw. "I love you, Beverly. But I need to know… are we doing this together, or am I just a safe place to fall?"

She turned slowly in his arms, eyes red but clear. "I don't know what I can give you, Bobby," she said honestly. "But I don't want you to go." In that quiet patience, formed a relationship born not from romanticism but presence.

Chapter 5: The Reckoning

The Millers' house buzzed with the constant need for attention by Beverly's toddling daughters. Their gleeful giggles stirred the rather deadened environment of Genevieve's house. The cling and clang of them throwing toys or any utensil or decoration they can grab. The never-ending patter of their soft soles against the hardwood kept the grandparents exhausted. The rapid tap-tap-pause, followed by a burst of cackles and squeaky shuffle, had Genevieve running after them all day long.

Penny and Jodie were bestowed with the greatest grandparents, but only when it came to spoiling them with toys. However, every toy, every gift came with an undertone of Genevieve's attempt to make the girls forget their mother. Though the toys were actually sent by their father and mother, Genevieve cunningly rewrote the tags and cards, portraying each one as a gift from herself. Genevieve's well-practiced consolations and love orchestrated a scheme of indulgence: keep the girls addicted to toys, new clothes, and everything glittery and shiny. Jodie's questions were met with reprimand, and Penny's bawling with disciplining tactics. As a disciplinary method, whenever the sisters made too much noise or became too much to handle, they were sent out of the house. Genevieve inculcated the approach of punishment from a very young age. At times, the sisters were sent out to walk to Chris Miller's sister's house or stand outside the house to maintain Genevieve's tightly controlled environment.

The constant poisoning of their heart and minds against Beverly began to showcase results. Jodie understood her grandmother would never provide her with any answer. Penny's tantrums and complaints dulled into silence. Gradually, Beverly became a distant thought for the two and four-year-old. It wasn't just the absence but a deliberate tactic of erasure. At times, Jodie would still ask about her mother before bed, but with no inquisitiveness.

It's just a matter of time, Genevieve forced a smile through her tight lips, closing the door to her eldest granddaughter's room. The younger granddaughter developed a habit of sleeping with her grandmother — a replacement Genevieve has been conspiring. Jodie and Penny grew closer to their grandmother and wary of their mother's tenderness. Over time, the seed of resentment Genevieve planted would soon sprout and spew bitterness.

***

June 23ʳᵈ, 1962

Melvin and Beverly had once shared dreams and a life built on hope, moments filled with plans for a family, laughter in sunlit kitchens, and promises whispered late into the night. But time had splintered that foundation irreparably. What remained now were two people, equally determined and exhausted, locked in a relentless battle for the custody of their two daughters. Their shared enemy was no longer each other, but Genevieve—the manipulative grandmother whose grip on the girls was tightening through bribes disguised as gifts and love masked as control. Both Melvin and Beverly, despite their deepening divide, fought fiercely to strip her of guardianship.

Then came the official summons. A crisp court notice arrived at Beverly's doorstep, summoning her to appear for divorce proceedings. She braced herself for humiliation, expecting Melvin to unleash his anger, to expose her infidelity before the court, before their daughters. But to her surprise, the filing was for a no-fault divorce. No accusations would be aired, no dirty laundry paraded. The law allowed neither of them to present evidence of abuse, betrayal, or neglect. There would be no villain named in the dissolution of their marriage—only irreconcilable differences and the passage of time.

Yet the heart of the matter remained unresolved: custody. Both parents dug in, unwilling to yield, each believing the girls would be safest, happiest, and most whole in their care. The courtroom grew into a battlefield of competing visions for Penny and Jodie's future.

The divorce was finalized on June 23rd, 1962, closing the chapter on a marriage that had unraveled long before the ink dried. And still, despite all the pain, Melvin made one quiet choice: he never let Beverly's adultery become the reason for their official separation. He could have, as the facts were there.

But he chose silence. He chose dignity. Not for Beverly's sake, but for their daughters' fate. He never wanted Penny and Jodie to look at their mother through a lens of betrayal, and never wanted their idea of her to be stained by adult bitterness. In his heart, he believed that no matter how their marriage had ended, the girls deserved to see their mother as nothing less than loving.

***

A few days before delivering her third child, Beverly's restlessness caused her to pace the tiny bedroom she and Bobby Orr owned. She was about to raise a new family, having no contact or information about her elder daughters. There had been no calls, no letters, no way to know if her two growing girls remembered her. Subdued gasps and sniffles punctuated the pacing steps.

Do they even remember my face? What if they forget my voice, my lullabies? What if they think mother is their actual mother? The longer she paced, the louder her sniffles and the more bitter her thoughts. Beverly's wonderment about her daughters clung stubbornly to her.

107

How can I take care of this new baby when I don't even know about my other daughters!? Beverly placed a hand on her round belly as if feeling the life fostering within her. She was unsure whether to welcome her third child, after all that was going on with her life and her new marriage.

Do they think of me as a bad mother? What if they think I abandoned them at the mercy of my mother? Thinking of this had provoked nausea and dizziness making her sit down at the edge of the bed. The squeaking of the old mattress awakened her partner, rubbing his eyes and trying to make sense of Beverly's inconsolable situation.

"Why are you up?" Bobby smacked his dry lips, speaking in a thick voice, "Did something happen to the baby? Why are you crying?" The worry about his child stirred him out of his somnolence.

Bobby Orr, though supportive in many ways, had completely given up on Beverly's search for her daughters. As the time of birth closed in, Bobby's complete focus was on the well-being of Beverly and his child — the older daughters were no longer his distress. Even though Beverly remained pinned to the plan of finding and contacting her daughters, her new partner paid no heed to it.

His days moved with steady calm and the joy of becoming a father. Whenever Beverly brought up the topic of her elder daughters, Bobby would quell her with a look. He would spend hours building the perfect crib, assembling the soft toys, and setting up the baby's wardrobe. He would give foot rubs to Beverly, time her contractions, make her soft meals, and even satisfy her weird cravings — his love present and powerful but selective. For him, the elder daughters were from another man, had a different name, and no longer fell under his scope of concern.

"Nothing is wrong with *your* baby. I am fine, just worried about my daughters," Beverly wiped her eyes, suppressing a sob. Bobby returned to his side of the bed, shrugging off Beverly's worry. As she lay down, she realized it wasn't just any other child awaiting birth. This child would probably break her heart into three — that her longing for the elder daughters might dominate her love for this child.

The day before Beverly's delivery, her belly had tightened, making the expecting couple rush towards the emergency department. The emergency doctor checked it out as Braxton Hicks contractions. However, upon Bobby's insistence, the hospital admitted Beverly on July 19th, a whole day before her actual delivery. In the late hours of the following night, the contractions resurfaced, and the warm gush below signaled that her water had broken. Her breath hitched, and her fingers dug into the swell of her stomach.

Despite the false alarm the first time, the second incident confirmed the urgency of delivering this baby. As she prepared for the delivery, her thoughts remained fixated on her daughters. While she couldn't wait to hold her new baby, she longed to hug and kiss her elder ones. The conflict brewing within rendered her hysterical.

"Miss Beverly, you need to push harder," the nurses and doctors demanded. Laughing and sobbing, all Beverly could hear were the cries, laughs, and giggles of the daughters she hadn't held in months, if not a year.

"Miss Beverly, you need to calm down first, else the baby could go into shock," the nurse whispered words of warnings and encouragement to no avail. Shivering, Beverly clasped her hands around the bed frame as if bracing herself for the emotional agony that exceeded her present physical toll.

"Almost there, the head is out. Almost. Just another push. Beverly, you are doing so good. You can do it," Bobby Orr cupped her tear-stained and panic-stricken face. Beverly gasped, her eyes rolled back into her head as she let out a whistling breath.

"She can't go unconscious now! We are there!" The doctor and nurses put her on oxygen and stabilized her body vitals while Bobby was told to help her calm down.

"Ha..py…bir…d..ay…J..di," Beverly's consciousness was retained before complete unconsciousness as she delivered her third daughter on July 19th, 1962, in Chicago.

Beverly was kept under strict observation and monitoring of her psychological situation. Bobby Orr and Beverly decided to name their little one Nancy Orr. The sterile room hummed with quiet tension, the monitor beside her bed ticking in the rhythm of her newly born child's heartbeat. Bobby stayed close, adjusting pillows, smoothing her hair, bringing her food, and reassuring her with soft words, love, and quiet strength. He would rock his little one to sleep once she was fed, play peek-a-boo with a few-day-old, trying to make her smile. At times, he would spend hours simply watching her sleep and the quiet cadence of her breath and coos.

A couple of days later, Beverly was discharged as her body vitals and psychological health showed no sign of concern. As for Nancy, she seemed to be breastfeeding with ease, her latch strong and instinctive from the first try. The pediatric doctor checked her for signs and subtle presence of any congenital defects and found none. Nancy's weight was healthy, and her cry was strong. Her tiny fingers wrapped around her mother's stray hair strand as Beverly exited the hospital with an awkward shuffle.

In those early hours of new motherhood, Beverly clung to every small reassurance: Nancy's steady breathing at night, the way her tiny body curled naturally into her chest, and the subtle, hopeful rhythm of life beginning again. She was stepping into this chapter with equal parts love and longing, carrying both the weight of her missing daughters and the light of the new life now entrusted to her.

For Bobby Orr, life had a completely new meaning and a different purpose. For him, keeping his little smiling, happy, and contended formed the core of his life now. Upon the slightest of discomfort or inconvenience, Bobby would leave everything else and attend to his daughter immediately, responding with mellow lullabies, patting, and caressing to make her feel safe. Gone were his days of idle distractions and multiple ambitions.

The few inches long, Nancy progressed incredibly. At four months old, Nancy attended her parents' wedding, though Beverly carried a deeper secret."Guess she could say she attended her parents' wedding," Beverly pecked Nancy's forehead, rocking her in her arms.

Beverly and Bobby Orr decided to have a secluded wedding in a private setting with only a handful of people as their witnesses. Beverly re-styled her old wedding dress, avoiding the expense of buying yet another wedding dress. Bobby bought a relatively decent wedding suit with a pair of formal wedding shoes. However, the couple bought a slightly expensive but absolutely adorable tiny dress for their four-month-old. The dress was styled with new shoes and accessories. Little Nancy would be the center of attention at her parents' wedding.

The re-styled dress arrived a couple of days before the decided wedding date. The sleeves were different, and the shape was slightly wider to fit Beverly's post-pregnancy body. Beverly twirled in her restyled dress, observing the length and flow.

"Wait, what is it? Is it…?" Bobby grasped Beverly by her shoulder, making her turn around to face him, "this is your old wedding dress, right? It looks like that."

"Don't you have an eye for detail?" Beverly put her arms around Bobby's neck. "It is, and I don't want to spend any more bucks on something I will only wear once."

Gripping her upper arm, pushing her away, and clamping his hand around her jaw, "Once, you say? But, this one you will wear the second time," Bobby spoke, grinding his teeth. His thumbs pressing on her cheeks, "You haven't forgotten him, right? You still love him, don't you?" The pressure on Beverly's face was unrelenting as Bobby's eyes continued to widen.

Bobby's nails dug deeper into Beverly's skin as she tried speaking. With watering eyes, she explained herself, "I only wanted to save some cash after the delivery and all. There's no other reason…" the punishing grip seemed to be loosening. "And if I wanted him, I wouldn't be preparing for my wedding with you…

I divorced him, Bobby." For God's sake, stop it….!

"You better not have any feelings for him, Bevs. You are the mother of my child. Never forget that!" Bobby stomped out of the room, leaving behind a completely shaken and utterly shocked Beverly. Though Melvin was her first love, the guilt she carried had long buried her feelings for him.

LOVE ME!? DO YOU KNOW WHAT LOVE IS!? Melvin's menacing words echoed in her mind. Beverly unzipped the dress, letting it cascade down as it pooled around her bare legs. *YOU LOVED THE IDEA OF ME!* Beverly gasped, exhaling the long-held breath. *…home is probably what I will never find or have,* she collapsed, burying her face in her hands and letting the tears soak the net of her wedding dress.

"Are you still in that dress!? Nancy is hungry, have her fed," Bobby's vexation made her leap to her feet and quickly change into her lounge clothing. She haphazardly stuffed the wedding dress into the zipped bag, threw it inside her cupboard, and locked it away.

Drying her eyes and wearing a forced smile, Beverly took Nancy from her to-be husband, "Thanks, baby. I will have her fed," running a hand into his hair, only to be rudely jerked away.

The wedding day wasn't as chaotic or happening as one expected it to be, with no caterers rushing around to set things up or decorators prepping the tables. Beverly and Bobby's wedding was a severely different wedding: refreshments were served, excluding dinner. he set up was simple, excluding the basic table décor and centerpieces, and the guest list was very brief, excluding the bridesmaids and groomsmen.

The ceremony took place under the soft afternoon sun in the modest backyard of a family friend. Bobby stood at the front, his hands clasped together as he fidgeted around, wearing a simple black suit that had clearly been tailored off-the-rack. Beverly emerged in her re-styled wedding dress, adorning a rather long veil, with little Nancy cooing and giggling in a pram.

There was no orchestra, no string quartet, just the chirping of birds and the faint rustle of wind through the trees. The officiant read from a small book, voice calm and steady. When Bobby took Beverly's hands, his eyes kept wandering around, never meeting Beverly's gaze. The vows were brief and rushed, whispered more than spoken.

When it was over, they kissed modestly. A scattered applause followed. Guests sipped lemonade and coffee, standing in small clusters. There was no cake-cutting ceremony or first dance, but as the sky turned amber and the shadows lengthened, the simplicity of it all felt strange. A beginning, not with fanfare, but in solitude.

The door to the Orr house clicked shut with a soft finality. Beverly Orr, Nancy Orr, and Bobby Orr returned from the ceremony to a dim, lifeless home—no balloons, no streamers, no welcoming glow. Just bare brick and looming stillness. The hallway carried the faint, stale scent of the coffee Bobby had brewed before leaving. The subtle hum of the refrigerator and the tick of the wall clock were the only sounds to greet them.

No garlands. No candles. No music. Just Bobby's shoes and socks, abandoned and crumpled on the floor.

Beverly gathered sleeping Nancy in her arms, parking the pram in the hallway. Anticipating a surprise, smiling, Beverly opened the bedroom and turned on the lights to descry a room with blazers, shirts, and undergarments strewn all over the bed and floor. The bed linens mocked her with a red wine stain bleeding through. Beverly placed Nancy in her crib and plopped herself down on the stool near her dresser.

"I thought this would feel different," Beverly spoke thoughtlessly, unclipping her earrings.

"So did I. But guess what, maybe that's all just made-up," Bobby unbuckled his belt and unclipped the suspenders.

Beverly let out a soft breath, exhaling in both exhaustion and disappointment. "I know what a wedding day feels like, and this doesn't feel like it at all. It's more like a 'silence before the storm' scenario." She undid her hair bun and tied the wavy strands in a loose braid.

Bobby chuckled and stopped before he could let out a laughter, "maybe because it is," cleared his throat, "… I don't think I know what to feel right now," dawdled towards Beverly, "We have been such a perfect fit, like lock and key that this mere paper documentation doesn't make any difference to me. I did it because I thought it was important to you," caressed Beverly's bare arms and inched closer, "look, this doesn't change anything — you will be my same old Beverly and I will be your Bobby. Unless you start to demand in that typical wife manner ..." Bobby tightened his grip on her arms, "Okay, sweetheart?" he pecked her forehead. Bobby went straight to the bathroom, pushing aside Beverly as if in a hurry to wash off the triumph of matrimony.

"Will you be quick? I have to change Nan…" Beverly's request was cut short with a loud thud of the bathroom door. There was laughter, no celebration. Only the steady dripping of the water from the bathroom shower, sporadic cooing of their newborn, and the silence between the two newly wed, echoing and deriding everything they vowed and had been sold in the name of marriage.

Beverly changed into her peignoir sets, putting in every effort to make this day feel like her wedding day before it ends. She piled the scattered clothes on the already-full laundry basket, changed and straightened out the bed linens and covers, and fixed her smudged makeup before Bobby was done with his shower. She switched on the bedside lamp, the soft amber glow darkening the piles of distractions in the room. She sprayed on Bobby's favorite fragrance, awaiting to please her husband. Beverly checked on Nancy, ensuring the little one slept soundly before positioning herself on the bed.

"You want to take a shower? The water is still warm," Bobby exited the bathroom with a towel wrapped around his lower body, covering what needed to be covered.

This is my towel, Beverly eyed the towel, without losing the charming smile she had rehearsed all that time Bobby was bathing. He put on the trousers, placed the wet towel on the bedside, and sat on the edge of the bed, the mattress dipping under his weight.

"Sweetheart…" Beverly's voice dropped to a murmur, soft and velvety. Her murmur requiring no answer but demanding complete attention.

"You undressed, so go get a shower if you want to; the water might still be warm. I turned off the heater," Bobby fluffed his pillow, buried his feet under the blanket, and pulled the blanket to his shoulder, lying flat on all the effort his wife had put in.

"No, I think I'll shower in the morning," Beverly put on her nightgown and lay beside her husband. Once the passionate lovers, now the two newly wed silhouettes, familiar yet strangers. *Is this the aftermath of marriage… this strangeness…* Beverly curled up, hugging her legs. *It wasn't like this with Mel… stop thinking about him,* Beverly chided herself, turning around to find her husband snoring audibly. *Did he really never want me as his wife, just a girlfriend?* Beverly lay flat on her back, staring into the nothingness of her newly married life.

"Why are you moving around so much?" Bobby groggily complained.

"I am just finding the right spot to sleep. You know I am a light sleeper," Beverly pushed off the blanket, her body warming up, not with the expected passion of the first night but the proximity of such insensitivity. After an hour of tossing and turning, she eventually reached for his hand and held it close to her face, not forcefully, not expecting anything, finding the comfortable position she was used to sleeping in. Such was the beginning of Mr. and Mrs. Bobby Orr, adorning doubts and featuring silence dressed in skin.

The next couple of months passed like a fog. Beverly tended to Nancy and Bobby busied himself with work, day work and night shifts. They rarely collided or even found time for each other. Sure, they made love. There was thrust, kiss, cuddle, force, passion, and desire; the contentment was tucked away in her reveries. Now, the only thing that remained was intimacy without the feelings, but with force. And this force and marital rape ended up with something Beverly could not anticipate.

Beverly was already 04 months pregnant. Her swelling belly pressed against the kitchen counter as she prepared bottles for Nancy, was a reminder of her becoming a mother, again. The heaviness in her body mirrored the dull ache of disappointment she tried to ignore, but could not as she was not aware of her condition back then.

On top of that, the unwrapped wedding gifts were the only reminder of their now-matrimonial bond. The thank you letters remained uninked.

Beverly held the test strip tightly in her hand before she laid it flat on the hand basin. A single pink line, then another pink line, faint but definitive. At first she was confused, but then everything began to make sense to her.

She sat on the closed lid of the commode, her hands clutching onto the robe. She didn't cry or smile. There was just silence. She just sat there and contemplated. She should be happy to become a mother again, but how could she be?

She would not have been happy to be pregnant again due to how she became pregnant, of how she suffered quietly from Bobby's abuse, whose behavior changed immediately after Nancy was born. Bobby's long working hours had conditioned Beverly, allowing her to put the baby to sleep before he came home, clean and cook before the click of his key in the door, and have herself all prepped up right after dusk. The routine was all they had in common or to talk about. Of course, words were exchanged, but they only revolved aroud groceries, appointments, bills, leaks, and cracks.

And just like that silence lingered dense and long, but nothing ever made it disappear.

However, upon further probing or even the slightest of coquetry, the silence was quickly replaced by expletives. The behavior of Bobby turned colder, and his words became severely toxic. Beverly never expected this from Bobby, the gentleheart she married.

After such eruptive behaviors, abuse, toxicity, and whatnot, Bobby had composed a pattern to assuage Beverly's resentment that only tested her. He would get her favorite flowers, bring home the fresh vegetables, make her her favorite meal, and do a couple of house chores, only to repeat the cycle and no apologies. No gratitude. Just empty gestures meant to keep the illusion of love alive. That became his pattern—surrounding Beverly's life with a cycle of silence, tension, and control, always followed by a fleeting show of tenderness.

There were hopeful days, too. Days when they laughed, teased, and tickled each other to tears, kissed and cuddled like young lovers, and had dinner by the candlelight. For a moment, it seemed like a lasting change to Beverly. But soon, they returned to the old pattern, the same routine, the same toxic relationship that had nothing to do with the other two girls that Beverly had left to survive to her mother

The days stretched on, exhausting and frustrating the two. At times, Beverly felt that her marriage would fall apart, only to be saved by a few words of loveless appreciation followed by what had now become the norm for lovemaking: thrust, kiss, cuddle, sleep.

Why is this happening again? Why always me? Oh, Mama, I miss you. I wish you were here to protect me, if only she had never taken me from your gentle arms. If only my heartless mother had left me in your care, where love still lived.

Despite longing for love, Beverly hadn't planned on telling Bobby about her pregnancy news. She was afraid of the consequences of the news. Despite this, she broke out the news in the middle of the conversation while washing dishes, while he sat in the adjoining lounge.

"I am pregnant," she paused, anticipating he would come and embrace her, like the last time.

"Are you sure?" came in response while he remained focused on the served food.

"Yes, the tests were positive…" she was interrupted before she could ask him to accompany her to the clinic.

"How did you let this happen?" Bobby inquired with his mouth full and spitting some of it on the dining table, "I asked you to take your control pills and remain cautious." "Did you not take them?" gobbling. Did you not take care of yourself? What the Hell is wrong with you? Where in this world does this baby come from?"

"I did. I mean, it is all too much, all too soon, Bobby. Maybe because of the one time you forced yourself on…" Beverly was gagged with a hand clutching her face and a fist grabbing her hair.

"Well, yeah, what were you about to say?" The plate clattered and crashed, "It happened because I did what? Huh," Bobby tightened his grip, yanking her hair harder, "I did what's my right, understood? I did what I wanted. You are no one to stop me, do you understand Bi***… and don't tell me you didn't enjoy it," Beverly stifled a wail, "You enjoyed it, slut, and you want no blame of it now." Bobby released his grip, leaving Beverly bruised on one cheek and slightly lightheaded.

"Well, nothing much can be done now. We'll figure out something," he cut in with a hint of finality to his tone, leaving behind only grief, anger, and isolation for Beverly to endure.

Nancy sat in her high chair, her face smeared with mashed food and eyes wide with innocent curiosity. Beverly forced a quivering smile at her daughter through her tear-filled eyes, making Nancy giggle, who tugged at Beverly's hair and rocked back and forth.

By the last weeks of the first trimester, her body started to change, the ankles swelled up, the hormones took complete control of her emotions, the body aches had her fatigued, all along with another infant, Nancy. By the time Nancy was crawling, Beverly's body was bearing more than the weight of pregnancy. On March 27th, six months into carrying their second child, Bobby struck her for the first time during an argument over dinner. The unawareness of her elder daughters had already exacerbated Beverly's mother's guilt, which now peaked with this new pregnancy.

How can I protect this child when I couldn't do the same for Jodie and Penny? The culpability of birthing the new life with no surety of its protection often rendered her insomniac. The once passionate relationship with Bobby had now turned into a slow-burning marital crisis, with Beverly bearing the struggles of pregnancy and the relentless demands and tantrums of Nancy. While

Beverly spent her nights feeding and calming their baby, followed by her morning sickness, Bobby would spend his nights out.

He would arrive later at night, smelling of alcohol and waddling like her. Often, he would find Beverly curled up on the couch, waiting for him, but the unspoken resentment had long replaced the joyous conversations. Every so often, the nights would end with a loud slam of their bedroom door before Bobby crashed on their bed. On those nights, Beverly would quietly wrap herself with Nancy in a thin blanket on the couch to shield herself from his forced love that felt more like ownership than affection.

The tick of the clock and hushed whimper of Nancy protested against the deepening silence. Then, there was the slam and click of the lock of their bedroom.

Waddling to her side of the bed, Bobby slurred, "Still playing the cold, cruel wife, huh?"

Beverly slipped into the blanket, pulling it to her neck, "I am really tired. Nancy was all over the place today. Good night," Beverly turned off the bedside lamp.

A yank on the blanket, the clatter of the broken lamp, and the ringing impact of his slap, "you don't tell me when it's good night. I tell you when you sleep." What unraveled after altering Beverly's perception of 'love is gentle.'

She didn't resist, because resisting only made it more difficult. Instead, she let her body go still, soft, and compliant.

Her stammered protests, 'I am still sore, I am not ready for this,' were quietened with a hand to her mouth. She turned her face toward the wall as he buried his in her neck, murmuring words that

121

used to sound like love, but now just sounded like trauma and sorrow.

The ceiling fan ticked overhead, and it seemed that time had stood still.

She closed her eyes, counted its turns, and waited... waited for it to be over.

Love is violent. Love is enforced. Love is ... not for me, she whispered as his so-called husband made his way to the climax, only to leave her in more despair.

Her ordeal had become her living nightmare that often jolted her up if she ever fell asleep. It was her personal hell, one that didn't let her sleep. A smack on the head, a bruise on her face, twisting of her arm, spewing expletives, and pulling her hair had become a norm to her — a warped kind of norm she no longer winced at. What troubled her was Nancy's presence during such maltreatment as a spectator. At times, Beverly's quiet whimpering would make Nancy giggle, too young to understand the pain behind the sound. And at other times, Bobby would mock his wife cruelly, coaxing the toddler to clap for the shameful spectacle he was about to inflict.

By the mid-second trimester of the 'accidental' pregnancy, the violence escalated. Bobby revealed a more oppressive side. From upbraiding Beverly for food, laundry, or housekeeping to openly disowning the unborn baby, Bobby was obdurate in not allowing this birth. A crying and moody toddler had become her personal failure as a mother. He had now started mentioning and talking about Beverly's elder daughters, not for her assurance but for her melancholy.

Finance, housing, and bills were his excuse to abort this pregnancy. At first, he would convince Beverly through his love-laden words and false promises. But upon her persistent denial, the convincing turned into regular confrontations. Whenever Beverly tried explaining how crucial it is to protect and love the unborn, a sharp remark about expenses would silence her request.

And if she dared say more, he would unleash his monstrous side on her and the child still growing inside her. "He never once referred to the unborn baby as 'my child', only as 'it.' To him, it was a burden, unwanted, a consequence of Beverly's supposed selfishness. Their arguments often escalated into violent confrontations. He would wait until Nancy was napping, then corner Beverly, unleashing chaos that left the baby frightened and unsettled. After his outbursts, he would pace the living room, muttering to himself, *'I'll take care of it myself.'* And eventually, he did, forcing Beverly into submission, making sure she understood that defiance came at a cost..

There was nothing different or special about April 10th, 1963; the confrontations doubled, and the conflict remained unresolved. It was an ordinary day at the Orr household, where screaming, vituperation, wailing, and scarring of toddling innocence. Beverly snuffled on the living room couch while Nancy had cried herself to sleep in her mother's lap. The man of the Orr household raged in the kitchen, banging pots, slamming the cabinets, and sneering derisions.

But then he stopped, the kitchen fell silent, and his grumbling now seemed closer. The footfall was followed by the thwacking of something metallic on his palm. The object didn't make much difference, but the look in his eyes had Beverly begging. She dreaded *that* look because it hinted that he wouldn't listen to any reason or justification. His grip tightened around the object; his knuckles turning white.

Beverly sniveled, "Bobby, please…" But his rage was out of control and malicious.

"I told you I will take care of it," Bobby stepped closer and seized her between his arms, locking her in her place with force to prevent escaping.

"Bobby, I will do what you want. I just need time…please." Beverly clawed her arm, her tears pooling around her chin.

"Oh, no, no, I gave you time, and now I am done waiting." "Now, you will see what happens when you don't listen to me." Bobby removed his arm from around her neck and pinned her down on the couch with the metallic object. He pressed it harder on her shoulder with much brutal force.

"Please, Bobby, I am carrying your child. Don't do this," Beverly spoke with controlled sobs.

"It is not mine! It was your fault, it was your choice! You did this," the diatribe was executed with a full-blown swing of the metallic object across her shoulders. She defended it by rolling over and down the couch on her back. Beverly stumbled back, catching the edge of the hallway with one hand as her vision blurred. Nancy stirred in her sleep on the couch.

Beverly blinked back tears, trying to focus on her breathing. She was trying to keep from fainting in front of him. However, her defence was met with a more raged attack as he battered his heavily pregnant wife with the metallic object.

"I AM DONE! IT IS NOT MINE! IT IS NOT MINE!" Bobby screamed, his temples throbbing. Beverly couldn't dodge the attack on her legs and arms… it was a mercy from him for not belaboring her back and belly.

"You think you're in control? YOU NEVER WERE! I AM!" heaving and perspiring, Bobby poked her waist with his sandal and left his wife shuddering on the living room floor. Before he exited the house, he threw the metallic object in Beverly's direction, narrowly missing her head. That object was a broken curtain rod.

Beverly slid to the floor, one hand pressed to the dull ache forming on her arm, the other shielding her belly. The silence returned, but it was no longer a reprieve. Instead, it was a warning to choose a different path for herself and her children.

She could feel it now, like a knot tightening in her chest.

The next time, he wouldn't hold back.

Chapter 6: Echoes of Longing

For so long, Beverly had endured the horror and the abuse. Now, with her fourth child nearly ready to enter the world, all she could think about was how to protect this baby while somehow finding a way to reunite with her two beloved daughters.

The loneliness clung to her like damp sheets. And each day felt like wading through a fog she couldn't shake off. She wrapped her arms around her swollen belly as if shielding the child within from the echoes of a past and the present that still bruised her memory. In the stillness of the night, she whispered promises into the dark. She vowed to safety, love, and a better life, not just for the one growing inside her, but for Nancy, too.

"I haven't given up on you," she whispered, unsure if she was speaking to her unborn child or the daughters she hadn't held in so long.

Genevieve's betrayal replayed in her mind like a broken record—taking the girls under the pretense of protection, only to tighten her grip with manipulation and deceit. Beverly had believed there might be a flicker of maternal mercy in her mother's heart, but now she knew better that she would never change.

Moreover, the abuse by Bobby had long taken her innocence, and she became a living victim, enduring the same pattern of abuse followed by a sugar-coated line of warmth, which means nothing.

The loneliness weighed heavy, especially at night. She'd lie on the lumpy mattress, one hand on her belly and the other reaching across the sheets as if memory could manifest her missing daughters. She pictured Penny's gurgling laugh, Jodie's messy drawings taped to the walls. Were they safe? Did they miss her? Did they remember?

Nancy deserved better than to grow up watching her mother ache in silence. Beverly had been strong for so long, but she knew now that strength alone wouldn't reunite her family. She needed a plan. She needed proof. She needed people who would listen to her and her cries.

But, there was no one around who would have believed her!

By early June, Beverly's body had swollen with exhaustion. It was showing signs of pregnancy. Each breath felt heavier. Each movement was more difficult. By the time Nancy was walking, toddling clumsily through their home. She sometimes fell, and other times laughed, not knowing anything about what her mother was about to experience.

June 11, 1963

And then, on a muggy Tuesday morning, it happened. Beverly's water broke.

Despite the hurdle, she made it to the hospital alone. Bobby had left two days earlier after another fight, something about bills, something about her "attitude." Beverly didn't care anymore. She was grateful for the silence.

The nurses wheeled her into the delivery room, and as she clenched the bedrails, her mind was elsewhere.

"Push," the nurse instructed gently. "That's it, Beverly. You're almost there." "Just a little push, Beverly. Push…"

Tears slid down her cheeks as she screamed. Her entire body consumed by fire and grief, and she felt the rip through her cervix. And then… the cry. A sharp, beautiful, shattering sound echoed through the labor room.

"Congratulations," the doctor smiled, lifting the tiny body into Beverly's view. *"It's a girl."*

"A girl?"

"Another daughter?..." Beverly sobbed as they placed the baby onto her chest. She was small, pink, and wrinkled, her mouth opening wide with defiance.

Beverly touched her forehead to the child's, trembling. "Diane," she whispered. "You're here. You made it."

Nancy was just eleven months old when Diane was born. Beverly never had a chance to recover from her last delivery before another began. There had been no rest between labors, only more fear. And unlike before, this child hadn't come from love or longing. Diane had come from pain, which was born of Bobby's rage, forced upon her in the most brutal of ways, that someone would never have expected.

The weeks after Diane's birth passed in a blur of exhaustion and survival, just like life had been for Beverly. Beverly's body had barely begun to recover when Bobby returned. He rarely helped with either girl, but he didn't mistreat them. His focus was always directed at Beverly. If she asked for help, it was dismissed. If she expressed concern about Diane's worsening health, it was minimized.

Diane cried often, and Nancy cried more. Sometimes, Beverly would sit on the floor, holding both the babies in her lap, rocking them with her whole body to soothe them for a mere second or a matter of minutes. Her arms ached too much to lift them. She hummed whatever lullabies she could remember, though the words came out as broken whispers. She was alone, terrified, and overwhelmed, desperately trying to keep her daughters safe.

And Bobby made sure she stayed small.

"You can't even handle two kids," he'd say as he passed her on his way out. "You're not fit to be a mother."

Beverly didn't respond. She didn't have the energy to fight or argue with him anymore. Diane was wailing in her crib again, another breathless, rasping cry that left her face blotched red. Nancy, not yet two, sat on the floor beside her, chewing absently on a broken crayon. The apartment was stifling. The air barely moved. The smell of sour milk and damp towels clung to every surface.

Beverly pressed a cool rag to Diane's chest and whispered soothing words she didn't believe. "You're okay, baby. You're okay." But they weren't okay. None of them were.

She was doing it all on her own now. Bobby was gone more than he was home. When he was home, he drank. When he drank, he raged. And when he raged, she and the girls bore the cost.

But once in a while, there came a façade of Bobby who suddenly transforms into a guardian angel, like the fairy godmother in Cinderella. He would show care and act like nothing had happened. Everthing seemed normal. But Beverly knew that this was only for a short time. This kindness was only ever borrowed time. Eventually, the ruthless Bobby would return, breaking through the illusion, his transgressions darkening her world all over again. It was a cycle she had come to dread, like the calm before the inevitable storm.

Still, she tried to maintain hope.

Beverly fed her two babies. Bathed them. Sat on the floor and sang lullabies until her throat gave out. She folded clothes with one hand while holding Diane with the other, while managing all other things. She hadn't slept more than two hours in a row in weeks. Her back ached. Her wrists trembled when she held a bottle too long. And still, she tried.

But trying wasn't enough. At least not when the world already believed the worst of her.

Nancy was teetering near the chipped edge of the coffee table. She was tugging a frayed blanket over her shoulder as she was fighting with it. Diane's soft cries began again from the crib. Her breathing always sounded like it was caught on something sharp. She would often wheeze, rattling in her tiny chest. It was terrible at night. And the Nebraska summer had made it worse, with its thick, damp air that hung in the apartment like a wet towel, heavy and punishing.

Upon the diagnosis, the doctors called it infant asthma. Or "reactive airway disease." They weren't sure. What Beverly knew was that Diane would struggle for breath and her chest would retract with each inhale. Her lips sometimes blushed from effort. While Beverly was trying everything to keep Diane safe from this condition, Bobby... he couldn't be bothered.

He drank. He picked fights. When he showed up, he brought more disruption than help. When Beverly tried to protect the girls or ask for support, the response was always the same: blame, insult, or outright denial.

But Diane was gasping. Day after day, her tiny body curling inward as if fighting for each breath, struggling just to take in enough air.

"You're just being dramatic," Bobby snapped once when Beverly rushed to the emergency room at midnight. "She'll be okay. You're the one panicking."

It broke Beverly every time she saw her little angel in this condition. She'd wrap Diane in a damp cloth, rock her upright for hours, and sing lullabies through clenched teeth while her own eyes welled with tears and overwhelming thoughts.

In November of 1963, Beverly was injured in a car accident while riding with a man named Melvin Collins. She was banged up badly at work for a while. Her ability to keep up with rent suffered. And, of course, word spread fast, which Genevieve had used to call her unfit for the children.

Still, after passing a few bad checks, Beverly managed to scrape together enough to cover some court costs and rent.

But things only got worse.

On March 23, 1964, Beverly reported her wallet missing. It was $142 in cash, ID, and a social security card. The police were suspicious and called her in on April 1 to take a polygraph. She collapsed at the station. Paramedics had to revive her with a resuscitator. Under stress, she admitted the money hadn't been stolen, but had been handed off to someone who had helped her in the past. She owed a debt. She was trying to keep her apartment.

Two days later, a former welfare officer turned police officer filed a petition. She claimed Beverly had no one to care for her children if she were arrested. That single claim, built around a false charge of lying about the wallet, triggered a neglect petition with CPS.

On April 3, 1964, authorities showed up at her door. Bobby was home. The airman at the apartment refused to let them in. Twice. The sheriff had to threaten arrest before the door was unlocked.

Nancy and Diane were removed and loaded into a car. Their clothes taken. Their toys packed. They were placed with a foster couple, Genevieve's best friend's daughter and her husband. They had no children of their own and were renting from Genevieve. It was no coincidence.

On the other hand, Beverly was arrested, charged with obstruction, and released on bond. By April 11, the charges were dismissed. Shortly after, Nancy and Diane were returned to her.

But not for long, as Diane's asthma worsened. The summer heat in Nebraska made her breathing unbearable. And at times, she seemed to almost pass out.

It was 2nd July, 1964, when Diane had stopped breathing for several seconds. Beverly had pounded her back, held her upright, and screamed for help even though no one was home. After a couple of minutes, the infant finally wheezed in a sharp, painful breath. With that, Beverly collapsed to the floor, crying harder than the baby.

131

That night confirmed what Beverly had feared for weeks. She knew that staying in Nebraska was slowly killing her baby. So she had to plan a move.

The next morning, she didn't wait for permission. She packed up what little she had: diapers, bottles, baby clothes, and one threadbare suitcase, and called her grandmother in Arizona and asked for a place to stay. The answer was yes, as long as she kept quiet and didn't bring trouble.

By mid-July 1964, Beverly and her girls were on a bus bound for the desert. The ride was long, hot, and cramped. Diane's breathing was shallow the entire way, and she would curl up in her lap, trying to sleep and play while playing with her hair, until she slept. Nancy sat beside them, watching the blurred scenery with wide, quiet eyes, clutching a stuffed rabbit Beverly had managed to save.

When they arrived in Arizona, it felt like a different world. The air didn't press down on her chest like Nebraska's had. And Diane, miraculously, seemed to breathe easier almost instantly.

Their new home was a modest house that smelled of cedar and linoleum. Beverly's grandmother gave them a room, clean towels, and little else.

"Thank you, grandmother," said Beverly with a warm gesture.

"It's okay, Bev. I hope this place works out for you," her grandmother said softly. The words felt hollow, more out of obligation than welcome. The comfort Beverly had once known with Lloyd and Edna was no longer there. This was shelter, but out of duty, not love.

"I wish grandpa Lloyd was here," thought Beverly

Though Edna had always loved Beverly deeply, she was no longer the strong presence she used to be which Beverly had once clung to. With Lloyd long gone, Edna had little power left in the household. And thanks to Genevieve's control and pressure from

Albert and Agnes, she couldn't protect Beverly from them, not anymore. The silence was enough to make Beverly realize how powerless she truly was.

Still, Beverly was grateful. She bathed Diane in a plastic basin, let Nancy nap on the cool tile floor, and did laundry in the sink. She started to hope. Maybe she could find work and could keep the girls out here, safe and far from Genevieve's reach.

But Genevieve's reach was long. And it was always hunting.

Within a few weeks, Beverly began to notice oddities. Strangers are slowing their cars near the house. Neighbors whispering after brief conversations with her uncle Albert. Her aunt Agnes showed up uninvited, always asking how Beverly was "really doing."

Then had their own suggestions.

"You've been through a lot," Albert said during one of his unsolicited visits. "Maybe you should see someone. Just for a check-up."

"No, I don't think I need it, Uncle," said Beverly.

"You seem sick, Bev," Albert said with suspicion.

"I'm not sick," Beverly replied flatly, holding Diane to her chest, feeling her tiny heartbeat. Then, with a sudden, swift response, she stood up from the chair and walked away from Albert. She did not want to see his face.

As she was walking past Albert, Agnes offered Beverly tea and spoke in the language of concerned betrayal. "We're only trying to help, Bev. Everyone's worried. Even your mother," said Agnes.

"Yes, right," Beverly replied flatly, not stopping as she moved away from both of them, seeing straight through their pretense.

That was the giveaway that Beverly was not aware of. Genevieve had sent her workers to do the job. And they had done it brilliantly.

On October 29th, 1964, Albert filed a formal petition in court. He claimed that Beverly had threatened her grandmother. He lied under oath. He said she had overdosed, had become violent, and was a danger to herself and the children.

With all the lies summed up like a wave, Albert accused Beverly of almost everything to prove her insanity and unfit for the girls.

"She is insane, your honor." "I request you to admit her to the Arizona State Hospital," Albert pleaded to the court.

"NO. I AM NOT." "You know that Uncle." "You know who has been doing it and keeping me away from my daughters," Beverly said with anguish.

There was a fire in her eyes, and she would do anything to protect her girls from the shadows of her mother.

Still, the court had some other plans. Beverly wasn't even allowed to defend herself, not even once, because the plan had already been in place by the mastermind.

There was no additional hearing, attorney, or anything. The judge had said it with three bangs on his table, "The case is adjourned."

Beverly's heart sank within her chest. She could not accept this decision after she knew what was awaiting her daughters. She could not let her babies live alone, without her.

"Please, they need me. I am their mother." She pleaded with tears running from her eyes.

"You cannot do this. They are the world to me. I had already lost my two daughters, and cannot afford to lose them. Please,"…

She cried for help. She requested the court not to separate her from her girls. But there was no one to hear her cries. And just like that, on the fateful day of November 2nd, she was admitted to the Arizona State Hospital for observation.

That night, as the sterile fluorescent lights hummed above her and the metal frame of the hospital bed creaked under her weight, Beverly begged them to call her grandmother. She wanted to let her see her babies. But no one listened.

No one told her that Diane and Nancy were already gone, that they had been taken again. This time, under the guise of state approval. But it wasn't the state. It was Genevieve.

Like the past, she had orchestrated everything. From the lies to the signatures, the transport, and the placement with the same couple, her best friend's daughter and son-in-law, Genevieve has done it again.

When Beverly was finally discharged in January 1965, the doctors declared her mentally sound. Her file plainly stated: "no psychosis." But when she returned, the room was hollow. There were no cribs, no toys, and no bottles. Her house, once filled with the warmth of giggles and child odor, had now become an unbearable place of silence and misery.

She ran through the house calling for her daughters, "Nancy, Diane, where are you?" But no one answered. Her grandmother refused to meet her eyes. Albert had disappeared, and Agnes was nowhere to be found.

Her babies were gone, and she was again facing the same situation she had when she lost Jodie and Penny to Genevieve years earlier.

Only this time, there was no illusion of misunderstanding. No one lied to her face. No one offered false hope. They simply let her return to silence. To a home scrubbed clean of her daughters' presence. Two cribs, gone. Toys, gone. Their blankets, folded and hidden or thrown out. As if Nancy and Diane had never existed.

Beverly stood in the empty room for a long time. She couldn't cry. Couldn't scream. Her hands hovered over the wall where Nancy's crayon scribbles used to be. They'd been scrubbed away.

She collapsed onto the bare mattress and whispered their names over and over like a prayer, begging God to give them back. But nothing came.

In the days that followed, she asked every question she could think of. Where had they gone? Who had them? What papers had been signed? Why was no one telling me the truth?

"Where are my daughters?" she kept asking.

"They're safe," was all her grandma Marshall would say.

And Genevieve? She didn't say anything or try to contact her. She didn't need to. Her silence was enough for Beverly to know that she had orchestrated everything again against her will to keep the kids away from her.

Every part of the scheme had Genevieve's signature on it. The false petition filed by Albert, the character smears whispered to neighbors, and the hospital admission that served as cover. While Beverly sat locked away under false observation, Genevieve made her final move.

The adoption was deeply deceptive and conducted entirely behind Beverly's back. It was a calculated effort to cut the final thread between Beverly and her children. Nancy and Diane were placed with the daughter of Genevieve's best friend and her husband, a childless couple who rented one of Genevieve's properties and owed her more than just rent.

They owed her obedience. And with Nancy and Diane, now in her custody, Genevieve had found a way not just to steal Beverly's daughters, but to place them with people who would rewrite the story, and never tell the girls where they came from.

There were no legal hearings where Beverly could speak. No forms to sign and no warnings. Just a sudden disappearance.

However, when Beverly tried to get answers from the courts, she was told there were no active cases. She would get to hear that there were no files with her name or no custody appeals, or any clues that would lead to her daughters.

Beverly was never informed that her daughters had been adopted. She lived the rest of her life believing Genevieve had custody of all four girls. After the heartbreaking incident, she drifted away farther and farther.

She moved through the world like someone half-awake, carrying bags of groceries she didn't remember buying. She often walked home to rooms that felt more like tombs. She got work when she could. She wrote letters that went unanswered. She memorized addresses she'd never visit.

In her mind, they were still out there. She could envision Jodie drawing with crayons on some stranger's wall. She could imagine Penny twirling in a dress that didn't match, but made her laugh. She could imagine Nancy would be cutting her first tooth. She could think of Diane, who would be struggling to breathe, and Beverly wasn't there to hold her.

Some nights, she convinced herself that the girls were all together. She hoped that Genevieve had them in some house where they could see each other. She hoped that Jodie remembered her enough to tell the others that their mama had loved them so much and hadn't left willingly.

But most of the time, she knew better that Genevieve would never allow something so kind. She knew her mother and her toxic nature, and she had experienced that Genevieve's love was never given freely and always came with strings attached.

As time passed, Beverly turned her pain into silence. She lived day by day with the hope that her daughters were safe and sound.

Beverly did not have stability at this time, but was constantly looking for work. She often finds herself a job that she could do, but her constant depression and the longing for her girls only made her condition worse.

Beverly believed that all four girls were still with Genevieve. She had no way to know the truth. And no one had ever tried to tell her, not even the court.

The only choice for Beverly was to accept the reality and hope that her daughters were safe in her mother's embrace.

Little did she know that she would have to carry this belief to the end of her life.

When Beverly passed away in 1997, she left this world without ever reuniting with her girls. There was no closure and no reconciliation. Her children, torn from her by manipulation and deceit, never had the chance to hear the truth from her own lips. And she never got the chance to see the women they had become.

But those who knew her in her final years remember a mother who still hoped to see her daughters one day, despite all that had been taken from her. That one day, her daughters would learn the truth she was never allowed to tell.

Chapter 7: The Cycle Begins Again

Grandparents are supposed to show love and affection. That was never the case with Genevieve. Jodie was only two years old when she and her baby sister Penny, just nine months at the time, were taken into the care of their grandmother, Genevieve Miller.

The circumstances were shrouded in manipulation and deceit. What was originally presented as a temporary arrangement (allowing Beverly and Melvin Hess time to get on their feet after separating) quickly turned permanent. Genevieve claimed the girls had been abandoned, left in an apartment alone, with Penny suffering from a severe infection.

But only Jodie and Penny knew that this was not the case. There was no warmth in the Miller household. Jodie got no hugs, no affection, and no encouragement. Her grandfather, Christian, was the only figure who offered some measure of care, but to a certain extent only, if Genevieve allowed.

Their uncle Ted or Teddy, who was fifteen when the girls arrived, showed only indifference unless they got in his way. With time, his cruelty surfaced without restraint. Genevieve, however, wielded her power with cold calculation. In public, she performed the role of a doting grandmother.

At church one Sunday, a woman in the pew behind them leaned forward with a smile.

"They grow up so fast," she said, nodding toward Jodie and Penny. "You must be so proud."

Genevieve turned with a gracious laugh and placed a gentle hand on Jodie's shoulder. "Oh yes, I've raised these girls since they were babies. Their poor mother... well, she just wasn't able to care for them. She left them for the sake of money. I couldn't bear to see them suffer."

The woman frowned sympathetically. "How awful. Such a shame it was."

Genevieve sighed, her voice lowering. "It's a long story. But I've done my best to give these little flowers a real home. Structure. Stability. Everything they never had."

Jodie sat perfectly still, her hands folded in her lap. She didn't look up.

After the service, Genevieve smiled and waved to the congregation while ushering the girls out quickly. Once they were in the car, the warmth drained from her face like a candle snuffed out.

"Sit up straight, Jodie," she snapped. "You looked bored through half the sermon. People notice that."

Jodie didn't reply. She knew better than to contradict her in public, or at all.

But, behind closed doors, she was critical, manipulative, and at times violent.

Throughout childhood, Jodie and Penny were expected to behave perfectly. Their role was clear. They need to be quiet, obedient, and useful. Genevieve often entertained guests and paraded the girls like trophies, then sent them upstairs with a bowl of nuts and instructions to stay silent. Their childhoods were monitored and molded to suit Genevieve's image, not their needs.

One afternoon, on her walk home from school, Jodie was struck by a van while crossing the street near their home. She was just five years old. The world blurred into sound and confusion as neighbors gathered, and someone ran to get help. Her grandfather, Christian, rushed outside to check up on her. He scooped her up and carried her inside to the couch.

But instead of concern for Jodie's well-being, Genevieve's first reaction was to scold her about the blood staining her cushions and shaming her for creating the mess. "Look what you've done," she said, her voice full of cold disappointment, as if the injury was an inconvenience, not a cry for help.

The girls had brief, fragmented moments with their mother, Beverly. There were family gatherings, pictures of all four daughters dressed alike, and even birthday parties with Beverly present. But the truth behind those moments was later obscured.

As they grew older, Genevieve continued to enforce control as both Jodie and Penny were expected to look nice, speak only when spoken to, and never cause embarrassment. Affection was rare and usually performative, reserved only for moments when others were watching. Inside the walls of that house, emotions were inconvenient, and needs were interruptions.

Ted, now a young adult, reinforced it further. The girls became responsible for peeling apples, gathering walnuts, helping with household chores, and even assisting on hunting trips where they were made to retrieve dead animals. Jodie, deeply sensitive, would often hold the animals and cry in silence. She was also made to shoot a rifle and was mocked when it injured her shoulder. Genevieve showed no sympathy, only satisfaction in her dominance.

Ted's abuse became more frequent and targeted. He mocked Jodie's appearance, threw objects at her, and involved himself in her private life to humiliate her in front of other boys. When Jodie protested or tried to express herself, Ted would respond with the belt, taking out his anger on her. Genevieve often asked him to "handle" her, reinforcing a system where pain became the punishment for having a voice.

School offered little escape. Jodie began cutting herself as a teenager and experienced deep depression. She was told constantly that she looked and acted *"just like her mother,"* always said with contempt. When she got pregnant at fifteen, Genevieve and Ted forced her to have an abortion and visited the father's home to ensure that no support would come from his family. Despite her quiet determination to carry the child, Jodie was given no choice. She was never given comfort. Instead, she was met with silence and shame, forced to live with her pain alone while Genevieve would dismiss her as nothing more than "a filthy child."

The punishment in Genevieve's house went far beyond harsh words or cold stares. It turned to physical, calculated, and always intended to instill fear. Ted became Genevieve's weapon of choice, especially as Jodie entered her teenage years and began asking more questions, pushing back in small, desperate ways. When Genevieve didn't like her tone, or when Jodie made the mistake of challenging a lie she had been told, Genevieve would reach for the phone.

"I'm calling your uncle," she would say with ice in her voice. "You need to be reminded of your place."

Ted would arrive within the hour, belt in hand, already pulling up his sleeves. "What now?" he'd ask, as if Jodie's existence was a personal burden.

"She's getting mouthy again," was all Genevieve needed to say. Jodie would try to disappear into the wallpaper, but there was no hiding from what came next. Ted would grab her by the arm and drag her into the living room or pin her in the hallway, wasting no time before starting in. His beatings were measured and deliberate. The belt, always swung with the buckle end, left deep welts that lingered for days. Jodie learned to clench her jaw and swallow her tears because crying only made her situation worse. Ted would sneer as he struck her, saying, "That's what happens to little girls who act grown," or "You think you're tough? You're just like your mother, loud, worthless, and disgusting."

Sometimes, the abuse was more public. If a boy came by the house to say hello, Genevieve would summon Ted to "deal with it." One afternoon, after a classmate came over to shoot hoops, Ted stepped outside and hurled the basketball at Jodie when she wasn't looking. It slammed into her chest and knocked the wind out of her. As she gasped for breath, he laughed and turned to the boy.

"See how that bounced off her?" he said, mockingly. "She's built like her tramp of a mother."

Jodie flushed with embarrassment, trying not to let tears spill in front of the boy. He left soon after, and Ted grabbed Jodie by the neck, digging his thumb into the soft muscle just below her shoulder. "Got a problem?" he asked, twisting just enough to make her flinch.

"No," she whispered.

"You better not."

Inside, Genevieve barely looked up. "Stop trying to draw attention," she said when Jodie passed her in the hallway, still cradling her arm. "You bring this on yourself."

Even when Genevieve didn't order the violence, she sanctioned it through her gesture and evilish silence. When Jodie tried to confide in her once, after a particularly brutal encounter, Genevieve waved her off and said, "Oh please, don't start it all over again. Stop crying." "You're not a baby. You want to end up like your mother? Keep playing the victim?"

Jodie learned then that pain had no audience in that house. She learned that there was no softness waiting behind a closed door. No apology. No one to say, "I believe you." Her wounds were both seen and ignored, and it was a cruel contradiction that made her question her own worth. Every bruise faded with time, but the shame and scars lingered to this day.

Sometimes, Genevieve would cut deeper with her words. "You're nothing without me," she would say when Jodie tried to assert herself. "No one wants you. Not your mother. Not your father. That's why you're here. And you should be grateful."

Grateful… that was the word used every time Jodie resisted and asked why she couldn't go live with her father, or why her mother never called. Grateful was what Genevieve demanded in exchange for survival and beating her up. And when Jodie didn't comply, the belt and the abuse came out again. The cycle begins again. She was locked in her room, denied meals, or simply ignored until she broke under the pressure of silence.

By the time she was fifteen, Jodie had begun to cut herself. It was the only thing that made sense, the only pain she could control. The red lines hidden beneath her sleeves told a truth no one else seemed to care about. One night, after another fight over curfew, Genevieve caught a glimpse of a healing wound on her wrist. Instead of asking what was wrong, she scoffed.

"Trying to get attention now, too? You think that'll make anyone love you?"

Jodie said nothing. She had stopped believing anyone would ask the questions that mattered. She knew that truth had no place when it came to her evil grandmother.

In the years that followed, Jodie endured a cycle of control, rebellion, and punishment. She started drinking, skipped school, and eventually ran away. When she did, Genevieve claimed she'd had a heart attack. It was a picture-perfect lie she had once used on Beverly as well. The police, however, saw through the act and gave Jodie a choice.

She refused to return home and entered the Freeway Station, a shelter for runaway youth.

Foster care followed, along with more instability. But eventually, Jodie met someone who would change everything. She was her final foster mother, Margie. In Margie's home, Jodie experienced something that she would never have experienced or expected. There was stability and respect for the first time. Margie was an ideal mother. She supported her through her studies, and Jodie was able to finish high school. Later, she got married and started a family of her own.

As Jodie and Penny entered adulthood, the doubts that had followed them for years began surfacing with new urgency. Why had they never lived with either of their parents? Why did every story from Genevieve feel rehearsed, inconsistent, or implausible?

The turning point came when Penny reached out to their father, Melvin Hess. What they learned shattered everything they had been told. Contrary to Genevieve's repeated claims that he had abandoned them along with the many lies about their mother, Beverly.

Melvin explained to them that he had spent years trying to locate and reconnect with his daughters. He shared legal correspondence, including letters from his lawyer to Genevieve's attorney, which clearly showed that he had been seeking custody or contact. In response, Genevieve's attorney had falsely claimed that the whereabouts of the girls were unknown. Despite knowing, she straight away fabricated a lie that was deliberate lie. Penny and Jodie had been living in Genevieve's home all along.

Melvin further revealed that each summer, when he made the trip to Nebraska to visit his daughters, Genevieve ensured they were nowhere to be found. Without fail, she sent Jodie and Penny to Arizona for the entire month of July. It was always just in time to avoid his arrival. What the girls believed were routine family visits turned out to be a calculated effort to keep them out of their father's reach.

Melvin had maintained a full file cabinet of legal correspondence and documentation proving his efforts to remain involved in their lives.

But sadly, the records had been discarded only a few months before Jodie and Penny reconnected with him. The weight of this truth was almost too much to process. Their entire lives had been shaped by Genevieve's lies and manipulation, and they were forced to believe the lies about her mother, father, and their lives.

When they confronted her with the documents and directly asked her why the paperwork claimed the girls were missing when she had them the entire time, Genevieve refused to answer. Her reaction was direct, and she simply walked out of the room, offering no apology or explanation. She had no sympathy or shame for what she had done, how she made their lives miserable and diverted them from her mother's love. Jodie followed her out, her heart pounding, her hands shaking.

Ted's daughter came out a moment later, offering only a shrug and an empty suggestion: "Sometimes you just have to let the past go."

But Jodie couldn't. Not anymore. Not after everything, because what had been presented to them was validation. It was a reckoning. Their father, the man Genevieve had painted as disinterested and absent, had tried. For years. He had searched for them, written to lawyers, and made the drive to Nebraska every summer. But each time, Genevieve had made sure they were gone. She made it sure that they were out of reach, out of sight. Then she would return and tell two confused little girls that no one had come. That no one wanted them. That no one cared.

It had all been a lie. The stories about Beverly, the so-called abandonment, the filth, the mental illness, the violence, were nothing more than narratives Genevieve constructed to justify her control and her manipulation.

Jodie and Penny had grown up believing they were burdens, believing their mother didn't want them, and their father had chosen another family. The truth was that both parents had been cut off. Isolated. Lied to. And the girls had been raised in a house ruled by silence, shame, and violence.

The emotional toll was incalculable. Jodie had lived through years of verbal degradation, where "you're just like your mother" was hurled like a curse. She had been beaten with belts, mocked by Ted, and told to be grateful she had a roof over her head. When she got pregnant, her body was taken from her. Genevieve and Ted decided the outcome, cornered her into abortion, and personally visited the boy's family to shut down any support.

Every act of defiance Jodie attempted was used against her. When she cried, she was told she was too emotional. When she rebelled, she was punished. When she sought comfort, she was met with silence. She had carried these wounds like invisible chains, thinking for most of her life that they were somehow her fault.

But now she knew better.

What she endured wasn't the product of chance. It wasn't miscommunication or bad luck. It was perfectly orchestrated and designed by the one and only Genevieve. She was the one who had written the script and played every part. From the savior to the victim to the villain, she was the culprit behind their fate and the years they have lost in vain, which especially Jodie, had lived in the wreckage.

And that understanding was the beginning of something new. For the first time in her life, Jodie had clarity. She knew that she was not a burden. She knew that she was not a failure or abandoned by her parents. She knew that she wasn't forgotten.

She had been stolen. And the people who claimed to have saved her were the very ones she needed saving from.

She couldn't let go of the reality. For years, Jodie had been told who she was. Now, for the first time, she was ready to find out for herself and for her mother.

And just as she was beginning to search for answers, one name resurfaced that would soon going to change her life.

Chapter 8: Finding The Truth

"Hi Jodie, it's Julie, I just wanted to reach out and let you know I'm thinking about you and I'm sorry if my contacting you guys has opened any old wounds, as that was never my intention. I was so excited to find you all that I didn't even think about how you might feel. My only intention is to get to know you. You are my sister, and I'm sorry for any pain or trauma you have gone through. I've always wanted to find you guys, but was deeply afraid of the rejection. But at this stage of my life and with the times the way they are, I wanted to try. So in saying that, I'm very excited and anxious to talk with you, but I also understand that you have to do what's best for you. If that means it will take weeks, months, or never, then I have to accept that. As long as you know I'm here, I'm open to anything you have to say with no judgment, and I'm available for you anytime. Please know I'm not Beverly; I'm not here to defend her or her actions. I just want to get to know you. That's all. Well, I've rambled on long enough lol, but I wanted you to hear it from me. My number is 602-396-8812, or if you want, we can 3-way with Nancy. I hope to hear from you soon."

In November 2022, Julie decided to take a DNA test through 23andMe. The decision had been years in the making, but it was shadowed by hesitation and fear. She knew what Beverly had told her, that "Genevieve had taken all four of Beverly's daughters, and that Genevieve harboured deep prejudice."

Julie herself was biracial, her father a Black man, and the thought of reaching out to sisters who might reject her for reasons planted long ago weighed heavily on her. The uncertainty gnawed at her, and she couldn't shake the confusion over whether she was taking the right step or walking into something she wasn't prepared to face.

The first DNA match appeared to be her sister Penny. Julie sent a message but received no reply. The second significant match, listed as a possible cousin, turned out to be Nancy's daughter. That discovery opened a door. Through Nancy's daughter, Julie was put in touch with Nancy.

The two spoke for hours… Nancy revealed that she and Diane had been adopted and raised together, something Beverly had never known, as she was forced to believe all four of her daughters were under Genevieve's roof.

Through Nancy, Julie found the missing link for her mother. But Jodie hesitated. The idea of contacting someone she had matched the DNA with sounds overwhelming. All her life, she had been told that Beverly had abandoned her and Penny, leaving them in an apartment for days without food or clean diapers. She had been told Beverly was unstable, unfit, and dangerous, and that Genevieve had stepped in to "save" them. The story had been repeated so often that it had become the truth Jodie lived by and believed to be the only truth.

Julie respected her hesitation, giving her time. But the need to connect was too strong to ignore. She eventually sent the long message that now sat glowing on Jodie's phone, hoping for a reply from her. Days later, her hope turned into a reality when Jodie replied.

Once they began speaking, the conversation flowed with ease. Despite fifteen years between them, they found uncanny similarities in each other. There were mannerisms, humour, and shared instincts. But with the connection came hard questions, and Jodie's anger toward Beverly was real and deep, fed by years of fabricated stories. Yet the mother she described was nothing like the woman Julie had known. To her, she was different!

Julie shared her own memories of their mother, memories of a loving, protective figure who had endured abuse, betrayal, and profound loss, yet she had never taken that pain out on her children. Despite that, her love for them was fierce, unwavering, and ever-present.

Together, Julie and Jodie began piecing together the truth. They uncovered the depth of Genevieve's manipulation, of how she had drawn in other family members like Uncle Albert and Aunt Pete, enlisted friends to pose in fabricated roles. They even used a woman known as "Mrs. Skinner," a supposed social worker who never existed. They learned how Nancy and Diane had been adopted by tenants renting from Genevieve, while Beverly was led to believe they were all still with her mother.

The stories told to Nancy and Diane were equally cruel. Diane's asthma, for instance, was weaponised against Beverly. False claims were made about premature births, abandonment in a garage, and drug use, all of which were directly contradicted by Genevieve's own written statement to the Arizona State Hospital, where she admitted that Beverly had never abused drugs or alcohol.

The more truth they unearthed, the more Jodie's perspective shifted. She began to see that Beverly's absence had not been abandonment, but the result of calculated and sustained interference. Beverly's efforts to maintain contact, letters, money, and gifts had been intercepted or disguised as Genevieve's own. They came to realize how Genevieve destroyed and diverted them from knowing all the truths, which would somehow lead to Beverly.

To date, they were forced to believe a false narrative about her mother, who, in fact, was a caregiver for her children. Not just for one of them, but all four of her daughters. Beverly had tried, time and time again, to fight the system, regain custody, and reach through the barrier that Genevieve and Ted had constructed around them like a fortress. But no one believed her. Worst of all, her children were told not to believe her either.

As Julie and Jodie grew closer, their bond became inseparable. What began as cautious messages soon turned into nightly conversations that stretched for hours. They compared notes not only about their mother, but also about the lives they had been forced to live apart. The similarities between them—their humour, their mannerisms, even the way they processed pain—were undeniable. Yet beneath the laughter lay an undercurrent of grief. Both were determined to uncover the truth that had been buried for decades.

Together, they began researching. They scoured archives, wrote to hospitals, contacted vital statistics offices for birth certificates, requested marriage licenses, and traced records through Nebraska's Children and Public Services. Adoption centres, newspaper articles, and school records became their evidence. Each piece of paper, each document, peeled back another layer of Genevieve's deception, and with every revelation, Julie and Jodie realised just how blind they had been kept about their mother.

The deeper they dug, the clearer the picture became. Beverly had not abandoned her children. She had written letters, sent gifts, and even money, but Genevieve had intercepted them all, disguising them as her own. Jodie and Julie realised that the very stories used to shame and silence them had been deliberately crafted to erase Beverly from their lives.

When Nancy joined in, the puzzle began fitting together more fully. Nancy revealed that after their DNA connection, she had reached out to Ted, introducing herself as his niece. Instead of acknowledging her, Ted flew into a rage. *"I am NOT your uncle,"* he screamed, ordering her never to contact him again. Later, Nancy discovered that Ted and his wife, Karen, had called Penny, accusing her of being the reason they had all found each other, blaming her for taking a DNA test. The cruelty had not ended with Genevieve's lies. It was a legacy that Ted carried forward with venom, abuse, and whatnot…

For Jodie, this behaviour was a continuation of what she had lived through under Genevieve's roof through all these years. She could easily recall the memory, which started with an argument about visiting a friend, which Genevieve refused with anger and rage. She cut off Jodie's request by giving no reason other than the familiar phrase, "You are not allowed to visit or go to your friend's house because I said so."

"I was the reason you are alive today, so you have to obey me"

"But Genevieve"…

"Shut your mouth. No means no"…

Depressed and out of rage, Jodie turned to walk downstairs toward her room, trying to put distance between herself to Geneieve. But, soon after Geneieve's cruel voice followed. It was sharp and insistent, ordering her back upstairs. When Jodie did not return, she decided to pick up a heavy wooden breadboard and threw it across the room, straight towards Jodie.

It missed Jodie's head by inches and struck the wall with force, leaving a dent in the plaster. She stopped in her tracks right away, staring at the mark it left behind. She was shocked and could not say a word, it felt like that time itself had frozen. The harrowing incident stayed with her not only because of how close it had come, but because it told her plainly what she had already begun to suspect, that if she remained, the abuse would only escalate to a point of no return. That near miss was the turning point for Jodie which convinced her she had to leave, soon…

Jodie never forgot the night of the breadboard. It was the moment she understood that leaving Genevieve's house was the only option for her survival, and to find answers to all her questions. That memory followed her into adulthood, shaping the way she saw her grandmother's rage, even as she sat years later in that hospice room in 2005.

In December 2005, as Genevieve lay in hospice from heart failure, Jodie sat quietly in the corner of the room. She asked her grandmother directly, one last time, where Nancy and Diane were, hoping that in her final moments Genevieve would offer the truth. But Genevieve gave nothing. She went to her death still pretending to be a righteous woman, still clinging to the role she had performed all her life. For Jodie, that moment cemented everything, which reassured her that no matter what happens, Genevieve would never admit her cruelty, not even at the end.

...July 2023

In the months that followed up, the conversations between the sisters became lifelines. Julie and Jodie spent countless late nights on the phone, comparing memories and piecing together fragments of their pasts, while Nancy added her voice and perspective. Each story and truth told revealed both the depth of Genevieve's lies and the resilience of the girls who had endured them. Be it the little fragments about Beverly or false claims and toxicity by Genevieve, the weight of decades apart pressed on them. But with every call, the bond grew stronger. The anticipation of finally standing together was overwhelming as they knew that the reunion was near, something that was stolen from them through all these years.

When July of 2023 arrived, the moment was bittersweet. They carried with them Beverly's memory, her struggles, and her love that had never reached them as it should have. For Jodie, the thought of seeing Julie and Nancy in person stirred grief for the years lost under

Genevieve's control. But, she also had a deep gratitude that, despite everything, they had found each other. Julie felt the same as she knew that they were not Beverly's abandoned children. They were Beverly's daughters, finally finding their way back to one another.

Then, at last, came the reunion. In July 2023, Julie, Jodie, and Nancy stood face to face as sisters for the first time ever. They laughed, they cried, and they mourned the years that had been stolen from them. Though robbed of a lifetime together, life had other plans, and now they chose to claim and take back what was taken from them. Now, they can claim the years ahead and uncover the truth about their mother once and for all.

Since then, Julie and Jodie have continued to visit one another, building a bond that can no longer be broken. Their search for the truth continues, but their connection is living proof that Genevieve's lies could not win forever. Together with Nancy, they hold fast to their faith that one day they will be able to reach their other sister, so that all five of Beverly's daughters may finally stand side by side—united at last.

Despite their story began with deception, now it endures in truth, resilience, and the unshakable love of daughters who refused to remain silent, no matter what.

Chapter 9: Restoring Beverly's Name

After their reunion, which Julie and Jodie had never thought possible, it gave them a second chance to rebuild their sisterhood. But as the initial joy settled, Julie, Jodie, and Nancy understood that finding each other was not the end of their story. Instead, it was only the beginning of a much harder task, which has more to do with their mother and the restoring of Beverly's name.

The sisters knew that Genevieve's lies had not just separated them, they had stained their mother's memory. To neighbors, churchgoers, and even to the courts, Genevieve had painted Beverly as a reckless, unstable, and unfit mother, who was nothing but a reckless and ruthless selfish woman. These stories had lived on for decades, repeated so often that even her own children had believed them to be true. For Jodie, unlearning those stories was a slow process. The breadboard memory, the endless commands, the shame she carried, it all aligned with Genevieve's cruelty, not Beverly's.

Julie, who had lived with Beverly knew a different woman altogether. She remembered a mother who worked tirelessly, who volunteered in schools, who ran Brownie troops, who made time to be present at every event. But still, her memories about her mother were cut short by her grandmother and her evil intentions to keep her and her sister away from Beverly's embrace.

The task before them was clear: to prove that Beverly had been a victim of manipulation, not the villain of Genevieve's invention.

The two of them began to work as though they were investigators, not just daughters. Julie wrote to the archives and requested records, and Jodie spent nights combing through adoption files, social services papers, and even newspaper articles that might reveal more about their mother's battles. Together, they pored over every scrap of evidence they could find to uncover the truth. Slowly, with time and their communal effort, the pattern became clear that Beverly had not been absent, and she had not abandoned them. It became clear that Beverly had fought many times to get her daughters back, returning again and again, crying and pleading for them. But Genevieve had no regard for her pain or her motherhood. No matter how many letters Beverly wrote, no matter the money or gifts she sent, every attempt she made to reach her daughters was intercepted and twisted. Genevieve turned each effort into a deception, carefully constructing a false image to erase Beverly from their lives.

For Jodie, the discoveries were both devastating and healing. All her life, she had been told that her mother left her behind, that she was unfit and uncaring. Now, with each letter uncovered and each record examined, she saw the truth with her own eyes and could not unsee it now. She came to realize that her mother had loved her deeply. It was Genevieve who had built the wall of lies around them. The resentment she had carried for so long slowly gave way to grief for a mother she had lost twice: once to Genevieve's lies, and once to death, that she could never recover.

Julie's role became that of a bridge. She had known Beverly personally, growing up under her care. She shared stories that reminded Jodie and Nancy of the woman their mother truly was: the one who ran Girl Scout troops, volunteered at school, and made sure her children never went without love. For Julie, it was painful to see how Genevieve's lies had erased that truth from her sisters' lives.

Nancy spoke about her adoption and what life was like being raised apart from Diane. While Jodie and Julie acknowledged her painful separation from Beverly, she has not fully embraced the extent of Genevieve's deception, partly out of respect for the adoptive family she loves. She is open to a relationship with Julie and Jodie, but she has chosen not to participate in the research or fully confront the truth about Beverly.

Together, the two sisters, Julie and Jodie, became partners in a reckoning long overdue, with occasional input from Nancy about her adoption. Like that, what had begun as late-night conversations turned into deliberate research sessions. They built timelines, cross-referenced documents, and shared every finding with each other. The work was exhausting and emotional, but it was also healing against every lie Genevieve had told. They now held a piece of evidence that disproved it.

As the sisters continued their search, they realized that their mission was not only personal. Despite all those years that they have spent in deception and falsehood, it was about time when justice should be served for Beverly. For decades, her name had been dragged through the mud, her character destroyed by those who sought control and knew nothing about her. For decades, Beverly has been a bad mother, a liar, and cast as the villain in her own life story. Now, her daughters were determined to set the record straight. They wanted her remembered not as Genevieve had described her, but as the mother she truly was—flawed yet remarkable, deeply loving, resilient, and undeserving of the cruelty she endured.

However, the process of restoration was not easy. Records were incomplete, memories were fragmented, and some family members still clung to the lies. But Julie and Jodie pressed on. Every document they collected, every conversation they shared, was another step toward reclaiming Beverly's dignity and grace.

Julie and Jodie grew especially close during this time. They had lost too many years to let distance separate them again, and each embrace reminded them that they were no longer alone and no longer silenced. Their laughter and their tears became a living testimony to the resilience of sisterhood and will soon prove to be the reckoning of their mother's love and fondness.

Looking ahead, the sisters knew their work was not finished. Beverly's story needed to be told—not just within their family, but for the world to see. They wanted people to understand the depth of her suffering, but also the strength of her spirit. They wanted her remembered not as Genevieve had portrayed her, but as the mother she truly was, as a woman who loved beyond measure and endured far more than anyone should have.

In pursuit of that truth, their efforts soon led to tangible results. Court filings revealed that Beverly had indeed fought for her children, filing petitions and seeking support whenever she could. Letters surfaced that she had written directly to Genevieve, pleading for updates, sending money, and asking for photographs. Gifts once passed off as Genevieve's generosity were, in reality, Beverly's heartfelt attempts to stay connected with her daughters.

The sisters also uncovered hospital records that exposed Genevieve's lies. The Arizona State Hospital for intense intake forms stated in plain language that Beverly had never abused drugs or alcohol. Yet Genevieve had spun tales of addiction, abandonment, and neglect, using those as fabrications to justify her theft of the children, just for the sake of money. The contrast between the official record and the family narrative was staggering and undeniable proof of the deception they had lived under for so long.

While Genevieve had gone to her grave clinging to her lies, Ted had carried them forward. While Nancy's attempt to contact him ended in his rage and denial, later, when Penny was accused of "causing" the sisters to reconnect, it was clear Ted still carried the bitterness and cruelty that had fueled their separation.

For Jodie, Ted's reaction was nothing new. He had long been the enforcer in Genevieve's house, wielding belts, shouting insults, and unleashing tantrums that reinforced the cruel message that Beverly was worthless and that her daughters should be grateful to Genevieve instead. Looking back, the sisters could now see how much of their trauma had been built on his complicity, his willingness to carry out Genevieve's will, and his hatred.

But they refused to let Ted's voice be the final word.

As painful as the work was, it brought the sisters closer. Each time they uncovered a new piece of the puzzle, they shared it immediately, piecing together their mother's life with more clarity than ever before. In doing so, their conversations were filled with both sorrow and relief, sorrow for what had been lost, and relief that the truth was finally surfacing.

And in doing so, Jodie and Julie found themselves not just uncovering the past but shaping their future.

The bond they now shared was unshakable. Julie and Jodie became the living proof that Genevieve's deception cannot last forever. Lies may steal time, but they cannot erase truth.

The weight of the documents, the petitions, the hospital records, and the letters could no longer be ignored, as every piece of evidence carried undeniable proof that Beverly had not abandoned her children, not even once in her lifetime. It became clear that she was not only a suitable and loving mother but also an epitome of resilience. She had fought for her children again and again, despite the obstacles stacked against her.

Beverly kept her daughters at the center of her world, filling their early years with laughter, play, and devotion, all while managing the responsibilities of home life on her own. Even as a young mother, she embraced her role without complaint. She expressed her affection openly and joyfully: "You are my whole world!" she would tell Penny, twirling her in her arms and covering her with kisses. With Jodie, she spun her around and laughed, declaring, "You are the love of my life!"

These vivid moments revealed her devotion and playful love. Yet despite her efforts, she was silenced by a system that gave power to Genevieve's wealth, lies, and manipulation. Like many women of her time, her truth was plain and real, but it was dismissed by those who controlled the narrative.

When Beverly was pregnant with her third child, her heart remained consumed with thoughts of her two eldest daughters, taken from her by her ruthless mother. The separation haunted her. Court filings, hospital records, and the letters that survived prove beyond doubt that she fought endlessly: pleading for updates, asking for photographs, sending money and gifts. Time after time, Genevieve intercepted these efforts and twisted them into her own lies.

All of that was buried for decades. But now it has finally been uncovered. For Julie and Jodie, these discoveries brought both validation and anguish. They had lived so many years under Genevieve's shadow, believing the false story that their mother was unstable and unfit. To realize instead that Beverly had been pleading for them, crying for them, and sending what little she had to stay connected, to unravel years of painful falsehoods in one crushing sweep.

Jodie especially carried the heaviest grief. For most of her life, she had been told she was *"just like her mother,"* a phrase weaponized to mean unstable, dramatic, or worthless. But now, seeing Beverly's letters and records, she understood that being like her mother meant strength. It meant persistence. It meant love that refused to quit, even when the world called it failure. The resentment she once carried gave way to grief for the woman she had lost, unfortunately, first to Genevieve's lies, and finally to death.

Julie's perspective provided the bridge. She remembered Beverly as a loving, protective mother who endured abuse, betrayal, and profound loss, yet never took that pain out on her children. Julie recalls her mother running Brownie troops, volunteering at school, and showing up at every event to support her children with pride and energy.

Sharing these memories with Jodie gave her a glimpse of the real Beverly, not the distorted version Genevieve had forced her to believe. What had once been fragmented stories suddenly came together into a clearer picture.

Together, Julie and Jodie came to a collective realization: Beverly's story had to be restored, for the generations that followed. Her grandchildren and great-grandchildren deserved to know the truth. And Beverly herself deserved to be remembered as the mother she truly was, resilient, loving, and relentless in her fight for her daughters.

Holding Genevieve and Ted Accountable

Though Genevieve was gone, her lies lived on, and Ted carried them forward with venom. When Nancy reached out to him, introducing herself gently as his niece, she did so with the hope of bridging decades of separation. His reaction was anything but welcoming. Instead of curiosity and love, there was fury. His voice, sharp and unyielding, was a warning, demanding that she never contact him again. In that moment, it became clear that Ted was not a bystander to Genevieve's cruelty but an active extension of it, determined to protect the lies that had poisoned their family for generations.

Later, when Penny was blamed for the sisters reconnecting through a DNA test, it was another confirmation of how deeply Ted's bitterness ran within the manipulation. Instead of acknowledging truth or allowing healing, he turned to blame and intimidation and further accused Beverly of hatred. He remained what he had always been: the enforcer. Under Genevieve's roof in the 1960s and 1970s, he had been the one called in whenever Beverly's daughters showed resistance or asked questions. He wielded belts, spat insults, and carried out the violence that ensured silence in the house.

For Jodie, none of this was surprising, as she was the one who had lived his abuse. When she was fifteen in the early 1970s, Ted and Genevieve forced her into an abortion, silencing her voice in the most devastating way possible. For years, she was mocked as "just like your mother," words weaponized to mean unstable, worthless, and dramatic. Genevieve's slaps and insults made it clear she saw Jodie not as her granddaughter, but as a mirror image of Beverly, the daughter she hated most. Together, Genevieve and Ted ensured that cruelty was the atmosphere Jodie breathed. Watching Ted's rage spill over into the present against her sisters, Jodie understood with painful clarity that Genevieve's legacy of cruelty had not died with her. It had been passed on, carried forward like an endless and deadly plague.

The sisters, however, refused to let that toxicity define them any longer. They agreed that accountability mattered as a matter of truth. They could not erase the past, nor undo the years stolen from them. But they could strip Ted's cruelty, and Genevieve's lies, of their power. By sharing their mother's story, they could reclaim their story, their mother's name, and their own voices.

They would not let Ted's voice be the final word. The truth belonged to them now. And together, they vowed they would not be silent.

Beverly's Vindication

The truth about Beverly's life and her motherhood was not built on rumor or wishful thinking. It was written in black and white, preserved in files, court dockets, hospital notes, and the fragile envelopes of letters she poured her heart into decades earlier. For years, those records lay buried, ignored, or twisted by Genevieve's voice. But once uncovered and read in full, they became the foundation of her vindication.

In 1964, Beverly faced one of her darkest moments when a false petition, orchestrated by Genevieve and supported by her siblings Albert and Agnes, claimed she was unstable and unfit to care for her children. It was a perfectly timed strategy. By branding Beverly as dangerous, Genevieve gained the leverage she needed to seize Nancy and Diane. Those petitions gave Beverly no chance to speak for herself, silencing her in court and confining her in the Arizona State Hospital while her babies were taken.

For decades, Genevieve told the story that Beverly had been institutionalized because she was reckless and neglectful. But the official filings said otherwise. They documented the lies used to strip her of her daughters. The very records that once condemned Beverly now became her defense.

The Arizona State Hospital files, dated late 1964, were supposed to prove her unfitness. Instead, they did the opposite. The intake forms included Genevieve's own admission that Beverly had never abused drugs or alcohol. Those words, entered as fact, dismantled decades of accusations.

For years, Genevieve painted Beverly as a mother lost to addiction, incapable of care. That false portrait was repeated so often that even her daughters believed it. Jodie grew up thinking her mother had chosen substances over her children. Nancy and Diane were told their lives had been saved from a reckless, drug-using woman. But the records proved otherwise. Beverly had not been addicted. She had not been reckless. She had been targeted.

From the mid-1960s through the late 1970s, Beverly's persistence showed most clearly in her letters. Time and again she wrote to Genevieve, asking for photographs, begging for updates, and pleading for any scrap of connection to her daughters.

In one letter she wrote of sending money and asked if the girls had received the small gifts she had managed to buy. In another, she asked whether they were healthy, whether they remembered her voice, and whether they still knew they were loved.

Genevieve never responded honestly. Instead, she intercepted letters, rerouted the money, and claimed the gifts as her own generosity. Toys and clothes that arrived at the girls' doorstep with Genevieve's name had, in fact, been purchased by Beverly—sacrifices she could scarcely afford, but sent anyway, because her love was greater than her circumstances.

One of the most staggering revelations came decades later, when adoption records surfaced. Nancy and Diane had been secretly placed with the daughter of Genevieve's best friend and her husband in Nebraska. The couple, childless and financially tied to Genevieve through rent, owed her their loyalty. While Beverly begged for updates and believed her daughters were together, Genevieve had scattered them strategically, ensuring none of them would ever know the full truth until decades later.

The gap between the lies and the facts was staggering. What had been called neglect was, in reality, manipulation. What had been portrayed as absence was, in truth, a mother's unwavering effort to reach her children.

As Julie and Jodie pieced these records together, they spoke Beverly's story aloud. They told each other the truths so no one else would inherit Genevieve's lies. They shared them with extended family and their own children, ensuring silence could no longer protect cruelty. And together, they began writing the book that would finally carry Beverly's truth into the world.

Beverly was never the villain. She was a mother who loved deeply, who fought relentlessly, and who endured losses that would have broken many. She wrote letters when no one answered. She sent gifts claimed by another. She pleaded with courts that silenced her. Yet she never stopped fighting, not until her last breath.

With her story now shared with the world, her daughters speak for her. They carry her story as proof of resilience, strength, and grace. They hold the documents, they know the truth, and they have seen the vast gap between the lies and the facts.

Beverly's vindication is written in the petitions she filed, in the hospital notes that disproved the accusations, in the adoption papers that exposed the theft of her children, and in the letters where she poured out her love. It is sealed in the voices of her daughters, who, after decades of separation, have come together to carry her legacy forward. No matter the cost, they will not let her truth be buried again.

How Beverly Would Feel?

As we pieced the truth together, we often paused to reflect on our mother. What would Beverly think if she could see us now? What would she feel about her daughters, once scattered and silenced, now standing shoulder to shoulder, carrying her name with pride?

For me, Julie, the answer was clear. My mother Beverly would be ecstatic. She would rejoice that her oldest and youngest had come together across decades of distance to clear her name from deception and falsehood. She would weep out of relief after knowing that the lies were no longer the final word. Beverly would be overjoyed to see Jodie's heart change, to watch her finally know the truth and release the resentment she had carried for so long under Genevieve's manipulation. She would find peace in knowing her daughters had found one another, their bond now unshakable, her legacy of love stronger than any attempt to erase it.

For me, Jodie, thoughts of my mother were bittersweet. I spent years grieving that she never lived to see this moment, that she went to her grave in 1997 still believing her daughters were lost to Genevieve. Yet alongside the grief came something I had never known before: a closeness I had long denied myself. As I sifted through the records with Julie, piecing together the truth, I began to feel her presence with me. Each document uncovered a new truth for me and restored my devotion to her love. With every step forward, I felt I was giving her the justice she had been denied, and in doing so, I began to carry her not with anger, but with love.

Now that we see the truth more clearly, we sisters understand that this book itself is an act of justice. We have no courtroom to turn to, no living abuser to put on trial. But we have our mother's words, her blessings, the evidence she left behind, and most of all, we have each other. Together, we could clear our mother's name for good and ensure her memory lives in truth, not in Genevieve's lies.

Our story will not be a tale of silence any longer. It is a warning and a message of hope. A warning about the dangers of unchecked manipulation, about how lies and power can fracture families for generations. And a message of hope: that love, truth, and resilience can break through the silence.

We hope this book stands as both testimony and promise to our mother, Beverly Ann, whose truth was buried under lies for too long. It is our prayer that by sharing her story, we not only clear her name but also shine a light for every family torn apart by manipulation and cruelty.

May these pages remind you that truth has power, that love endures beyond betrayal, and that resilience can be carried across generations. Our mother's life was an epitome of her strength, her love, and her unbreakable bond with us. And now, as she is no longer here to tell her story, we are her voice.

At last, the world will know her as she truly was. The world will know the truth about Beverly.

This is the only known photograph of Beverly's four daughters together. Believed to have been taken during a holiday visit in the early 1960s, when the adoptive parents were renting a home from Genevieve. Though their lives were divided, this single image endures as quiet evidence that, for one fleeting moment, they stood together as sisters.

Reflections from Those Who Knew Beverly

Beverly's story does not end with the voices of her daughters alone. Those who knew her during her lifetime remember her warmth, humor, and generosity. These reflections, shared by friends and family who experienced her love firsthand, offer a glimpse of the woman she truly was: the mother, grandmother, and friend whose kindness reached far beyond her own home.

From Latreasa Barbour

"When I was a little girl, your mom always called me Lil Dewan or Lil Red. We played with you and your brother across the street, always at Mr. and Mrs. Cherry's house. Every time she saw me, her face lit up, and she'd say, 'Hey there, does your mother or grandfather know you over here playing?' I'd smile back and say no, but I'd tell them later. She was always kind to me and my sister—we were like family. She was also my Brownie and Girl Scout leader. She loved us, and we loved her.

From Flisha Reese

"I want to thank Grandma Beverly for always showing me love. As a child, I was always excited to see her driving down the street in her ice cream truck. She would stop and give me, my sisters, and my cousins free candy because we were her grandchildren. I'll never forget her beautiful long red hair. I miss her dearly and feel truly blessed to have known her."

From Shavitta Martin

"I met Julie in 1993, and I've had the pleasure of being part of this family for over 30 years. Miss Bev was always nice and friendly to me—the first person I ever met who had pet rabbits, which I thought was so cute. She loved her family with her whole heart and would do whatever she could for her kids and grandkids. She had a special bond with her oldest grandson, Jordan. The love between them could be felt in your soul. Miss Bev was a strong and loving anchor for her family. She is truly missed by all who knew her."

These words confirm what we always knew: Beverly Ann Martin Hess was never the villain, but the heart of every home she touched. These voices reflect the truth our beloved mother lived every day. She was love in motion. She was a true beauty with grace and devotion. Whether as a mother, grandmother, mentor, or neighbor, through these reflections, Beverly's warmth continues to shine, reminding us that kindness outlives cruelty, and love always leaves traces that even lies cannot erase.

Dedication to Beverly

To our beloved mother, Beverly

We, your daughters, Julie and Jodie, carry your name, your story, and your love in every breath of our lives. Though you endured cruelty and loss beyond what any mother should, you never stopped loving us, never stopped fighting for us, and never stopped believing in the bond between a mother and her children.

For years, your truth was hidden under lies and manipulation created by Genevieve, but today, we stand as your voice. We dedicate these words, these pages, and this story to you, our beloved mother. Without your strength, we would never be here to tell the truth.

May the world know you not for the slander that was spoken, but for the love you gave and the strength you embodied.

Mama, we love you. We honor you. And we promise that your truth will never again be silenced, again.

Thank you… with all our hearts,

Julie & Jodie

A Final Message of Hope

This book is both our testimony and our warning. It is a testimony to our mother, Beverly Ann Martin Hess, whose voice was stolen but not erased. And it is a warning about the destructive power of manipulation, abuse, and deceit, and what happens when someone steals the softness of a mother's love from your life.

These forces can fracture families, steal childhoods, and leave scars that reach across generations. Be it the many lies, when repeated often enough, these false allegations can trap the innocent and vulnerable in cages of silence and shame, like it shaped our mother's identity…

But just as darkness gives way to light, our story is also about resilience. It proves that truth, no matter how long it is buried, will rise. It shows that love is stronger than cruelty, and that even after decades of separation, the bond between a mother and her children can endure. With the support of each other and the blessing of our mother, who is now in heaven, we have learned that resilience means more than survival. It means choosing to confront lies, uncover evidence, and speak the truth out loud, even when others would rather keep it hidden.

We hope that every one of you who reads this book, who walks through these pages, carries away both the caution and the hope. We pray and hope that you will be vigilant with the stories you are told. Question what does not feel right? Protect your families with compassion, and never underestimate how far manipulation can reach when left unchecked. Despite how dark and miserable your life may seem, you need to know that silence can be broken, healing is possible, and love can still restore what was stolen.

This book is our act of justice. It is our mother's vindication. And it is also our call to you to never allow silence to cover injustice, never allow manipulation to define truth, and never let cruelty have the final word.

Above all, it is a conviction from our mother, **Beverly**, to never let hope slip from your finger and to find healing in the truth. It is a message for every mother who may be struggling through her own battles, and for every child like us who longs for the love of a mother.

We hope that you may soon find the love and grace you deserve, and that one day, Penny and Diane will join us in this truth. We believe that one day soon, love will bring us all together. And when it does, our circle will finally be whole, just as our mother always dreamed it would be. We hope that these pages remind you that our mother never stopped fighting for us, that her love never wavered, and that her daughters, though separated, were always bound by the same unbreakable thread.

With love and truth, from Julie & Jodie

Julie and Jodie, united after more than sixty years of separation. What began as a DNA search turned into a journey of truth and healing, and the enduring love of the mother who never stopped believing in them. Today, Julie and Jodie are happy to have found each other and to finally share the bond that was always meant to be.

They remain hopeful that one day, all 5 of Beverly's daughters will be united.

.

Appendix: Evidence and Artifacts

Letter from Beverly, 1961 (Chicago, Illinois)

The following are Beverly's handwritten letter to her mother, dated October 27, 1961. From a small apartment in Chicago, she wrote of working at a factory, sending money home, and begging to see her daughters. Her words show a mother who never stopped trying to reconnect, even when every door was closed.

> Chicago, Ill.
> October 27, 1961.
>
> My Dearest Jodie, Genny - Mom,
>   Dad + Eddie -
>   I received your letter. I was
> so glad to hear from you.
> Also was so proud to get
> a picture of my babies.
> was so sorry to hear they
> were sick. I hope by now
> they are better.
>   Mom - the reason I never
> wrote the last three weeks is
> that I was under the impression
> you didn't care whether I wrote
> or not.
>   In the last letter I wrote,
> I asked for some pictures of
> the babies and their clothes
> sizes. You didn't send either
> Also your letter sounded kind

of snotty. I'm sending some money for the kids support. I have found a better job. I'm working for Motorola T.V. Manufacturing. I'm a machine operator. I've been there a month Monday. I also get a raise Monday to $1.82 hr. so maybe then I can get more money to the kids. You know its not to easy to keep two seperate places with money.

It would be so much better if the babies were here. But I guess you & Mrs. Skinner just don't want that.

I'm sorry about your hands. I suppose that I'm being blamed for that too. But if anyones going to get the blame, I suppose it might as well be me.

it doesn't seem like you
want me to have them.
I'm saving now so I can
come home for Xmas to
be with them and you. That
is if you want me.
Mom — I want you to
tell Joan that her mommy
loves her very much. Tell
her Mommy will be home
Xmas to see her. Oh yes tell
mrs. Skinner I kept a
stub off the Money Order, and
that the reason I sent it
straight to you is because
you needed it right away.
Tell her I will send the
money from now on to her.
Well I better close for
now. Please give my
babies a big kiss from
their mommy. Also tell Eddie
I'm sorry I didn't get

179

As about my getting a divorce
no I haven't I'm getting it
on the 2 yrs. separation. I've
just have 8 mo's to go.
As for me getting Melvin
to help with support money—
the lawyer said I couldn't
make him pay support
until the babies are back in
my custody. So its up to Mrs.
Skinner to get him to pay.
You asked why I didn't
care about the babys. Mom—
my babies mean more to me
than anything in this world.
Don't you think I'd like to
come and see them? I
cry myself to sleep every
night wanting them. But

to get him a birthday present
but I'll get him a double
Xmas present.

See Dad I said hi and
I hope he's feeling okay.

Mom, if the babies need
any winter clothes at all
please send me their clothes
sizes, okay?

Oh yes. If you get a
chance please call Mrs.
Skinner and ask her just
what I have to do to get
my babies with me? She
said when I was there
I had to prove I could care
for the babies but I was
trying. Well the investigator
here told me she didn't
see any reason why I
shouldn't have them with me,

181

I was sending money and really trying and what good did it do me. All she did was write saying she didn't think I was ready to have them. No reason or anything.

So please call her and ask just what I have to do to get them.

Well I guess I had better close for now.

With love to all,
Beverly

P.S. Write soon. If you have any more pictures of the tables, please send them. I have the last ones enlarged and framed.

Bye now.

Mom, I am sending a
pr. of shoes. If ~~Gudie~~
can't wear them, ~~have~~
them for Gene Jr. they
are good shoes. A woman
at work paid $7.98 for
them for her baby and
they were too ~~small so~~
she sold them to me.

I know this money
isn't much. But ~~will~~ try
to send ~~more~~ next time.
Okay? ~~~~

$4.00 of it is for the
babies. Let them each
pick out 50¢ worth of
toys or candy.

Oh yes- Since I
changed jobs I had to
have my mail come

else where. My new
address is

~~Mrs Beverly Gess~~
~~P.O. Box 106~~
~~River Mills, Ill~~

The cards are some I
got where I worked
before. I thought maybe
the babies would like
to play with them.
If you have any
more pictures of all
of you, send me some.
Well must close
now.

Love to all,
Beverly

Papers Records – 1963 to 1964

The following are the newspaper clippings from *The Lincoln Journal Star* and *The Daily Reporter (Lincoln, Nebraska)* confirm the violence and injustice surrounding Beverly's life.

• 1963 – Bobby Orr charged with "Assault with Intent to Do Great Bodily Harm."

• 1964 – Fire-station report notes Beverly's resuscitation at police precinct.

• April 1964 – Charge of "Obstructing and Perverting Justice," later dismissed.

Together these public records disprove the myths of instability and neglect, showing instead a woman enduring and surviving.

NEW CASES

MARCH 15

82-21 State v Stanley Laven issue check with intent to defraud, dism

82-66 State v Henry R Aspedon issue check with intent to defraud, pg $10

E22496 Frank Wahl pet to determine inheritance tax, vol apprnc & waiver, Davis, Thone, Bailey & Polsky

82-68 State v Bobby Orr assault with intent to do great bodily injury, Apr 10, bond $3000

MARCH 16

82-70 State v Douglas L LaPage burglary, bound over to Dist Ct, bond $2000 gv

82-69 State v Michael C Glenn burglary, bound over to Dist Ct, bond $2000 gv

MARCH 18

G6613 Henry Schwetzer pet for gdn (Mar 2), ord h

E22484 Elizabeth Maude Judge pet to prob will, (Mar 12), ord h, not, Lester L Dunn

E22405 Benjamin H Grant pet to

186

Lincoln Journal Star (Lincoln, Nebraska) · Wed, Mar 27, 1963 · Page 31

Printed on Jan 8, 2023

COURTS

All guilty unless indicated. All Municipal Court unless indicated as County (CC) District (DC) or Federal (FC) Court costs in addition to fine amounts. Municipal Judges John Jacobson and Richard O. Johnson, Co. Judge Ralph Slocum; District Judge Elmer Scheele and Federal Judge Robert Van Pelt.

Assault with Intent to do Great Bodily Harm

Orr, Bobby—26, 220 So. 26th, (allegedly assaulted Beverly Orr), waived preliminary hearing, bound to District Court, $2,500 bond. (CC).

Contributing to Child's Neglect

Wolfgang, Richard—25, 1644 E, (allegedly neglected child,), re-

187

Lincoln Journal Star (Lincoln, Nebraska) · Thu, Apr 25, 1963 · Page 27

Printed on Jan 8, 2023

COURTS

All guilty unless indicated. All Municipal Court unless indicated as County (CC), District (DC) or Federal (FC). Court costs in addition to fine amounts. Municipal Judges John Jacobson and Richard O. Johnson, Co. Judge Ralph Slocum; District Judge Herbert Ronin and Federal Judge Robert Van Pelt.

Assault to Do Great Bodily Injury

Orr, Bobby — 26, 220 So. 26th, (allegedly assaulted Beverly Orr), innocent plea, amended to assault and battery, pleaded guilty, sentence deferred pending probation officer's investigation, held in jail. (DC).

Burglary

NEW CASES

JANUARY 23

G6764 Fannie B McCrea pet for gdn, ord h, John H Comstock

JANUARY 29

90-186 Mary E DeJarnett v Gene Coltier money loaned & for services $763.50, Carl H Petedson

JANUARY 31

82-1163 State v Beverly Ann Orr insufficient fund check, png, Feb 13, bond $200 gv

80-879 State v Leonard A Bockhoven littering, pg, found not guilty, dism

82-1172 State v Lawrence E Johnson obtain goods by false pretenses, pg $50

82-1171 State v Donald E Zachek pet larceny, pg, sentence deferred to Feb 7

FEBRUARY 1

FIRE CALLS
Wednesday

3:00 a.m., 3071 U, home of Eileen Blodgett, bed afire, damage estimated at less than $50.

6:55 a.m., 144 So. 11th, apartments, bed afire, damage estimated at less than $150.

8:24 a.m., 3036 N, overheated furnace motor, damage estimated at less than $50.

10:56 a.m., 815 Judson, grass fire, no damage.

11:18 a.m., 814 Nelson, grass fire, no damage.

11:42 a.m., 1525 Sunburst Lane, trash fire out of control, no damage.

12:16 p.m., 505 So. 14th, woman locked out of apartment, no fire, no damage.

6:07 p.m., 323 No. 10th, resuscitator used five minutes on Beverly Orr, illness.

11:03 p.m., 2122 Stockwell, overheated furnace motor, no damage.

11:38 p.m., 5818 J, car owned by Norman Smith, short in wiring, damage estimated at less than $50.

190

FIRE RUNS
Wednesday

3:00 a.m., 3071 U, bedding fire.

6:55 a.m., 144 So. 11th, apartment, bedding afire.

8:29 a.m., 3036 N, furnace motor.

10:56 a.m., 815 Judson, grass fire.

11:18 a.m., 814 Nelson, grass fire.

11:42 a.m., 1525 Sunburst Lane, trash fire.

12:16 p.m., 505 So. 14th, defective lock, no fire.

6:07 p.m., at police staion, resuscitator used on Beverly Orr, 24, 1030 K.

11:03 p.m., 2122 Stockwell, overheated furnace.

The Lincoln Star (Lincoln, Nebraska) · Sat, Apr 11, 1964 · Page 19

Printed on Jan 8, 2023

COUNTY COURT

Note: All cases heard by Judge Ralph Slocum.

Misdemeanors

ASSAULT AND BATTERY—Pat Scott, of 27th and Cornhusker, pleaded innocent March 18, trial held, found innocent.

OBSTRUCTING AND PERVERTING JUSTICE—Beverly Ann Orr, of 1030 K, pleaded innocent April 3, case dismissed at request of county attorney.

DISTURBING THE PEACE — Hurley Francisco, 45, of 3160 W, pleaded guilty, fined $25.

Felonies

NO FUND CHECK—Kenneth Miller, no

192

Letter from Melvin Hess's Attorney, 1973

Dated November 28, 1973, this letter from attorney E. Craig Carretta to the Lancaster County Attorney shows Melvin Hess's ongoing efforts to find and support his daughters.

He offered $85 per month in child support and asked for contact information and visitation rights—proof that Beverly and Melvin never abandoned their children but were kept apart by deception.

CARRETTA, CARTWRIGHT & GILL

ATTORNEYS AT LAW

913/879-2281

E. Craig Carretta
Richard Cartwright
James F. Gill
—

35 N. Broad St., Fairborn, Ohio 45324

November 28, 1973

Mr. Douglas McClain
Deputy County Attorney
Lancaster County Attorney's Office
County-City Building
Lincoln, Nebraska 68508

Re: HESS, Mel -v- HESS, Beverly
    Case No. 35275
    [CCG # 73 573]

Dear Mr. McClain:

I represent the above indicated Melvin Hess. Enclosed is a copy of a letter that Mr. Hess received from your office earlier this month. Also enclosed is a copy of the DIVORCE DECREE filed between the parties in 1962.

Since the COURT ORDER indicates that the issue of support in the Court of primary jurisdiction has been reserved, Mr. Hess has not been in violation of law during the years since 1962.

Mr. Hess recognizes an obligation to his children and is eager to re-establish contact with them. It is our desire at this time to negotiate a settlement concerning support obligation. Before this matter is finally determined, however, it will be necessary for Mr. Hess to receive through my office specific information concerning the address, telephone number, and condition of the minor childre. Issues of visitation should also be discussed at this time and we propose an agreed entry to be signed by the parties and filed in the Court of Common Pleas, Greene County, Ohio, Case Number 35275 concerning not only the support, but also visitation between Mr. Hess and his children.

I am prepared to offer at this time the sum of Eighty-five Dollars ($85.00) per month in child support.

Mr. Douglas McClain
Page Two
November 28, 1973

I would suggest that this letter constitutes tender
of that amount on a monthly basis to commence with our
receipt of the information concerning the whereabouts of
the children requested above.

Thank you for your assistance.

Sincerely,

E. Craig Carretta

ECC:sst
Enclosure
cc: Mr. Mel Hess
    150 Circle Drive
    Fairborn, Ohio   45324

Childhood & Family Photos

Beverly with her grandfather, Lloyd Marshall, in 1943. She was just three years old. Lloyd, a decorated Army veteran, was one of the few sources of stability and unconditional love in her early life. This quiet moment captures the safety she knew before Genevieve reclaimed her.

Beverly as a young girl with Genevieve, Christian Miller, and Ted, in Denton, Nebraska, circa 1946. This photo was supposedly taken right after Beverly was taken from her grandparents, Lloyd and Edna Marshall.

Six-year-old Beverly holding her favourite doll on her birthday, given to her by grandpa. This photo captures one of her last joyful moments before being taken from her grandparents to live with Genevieve.

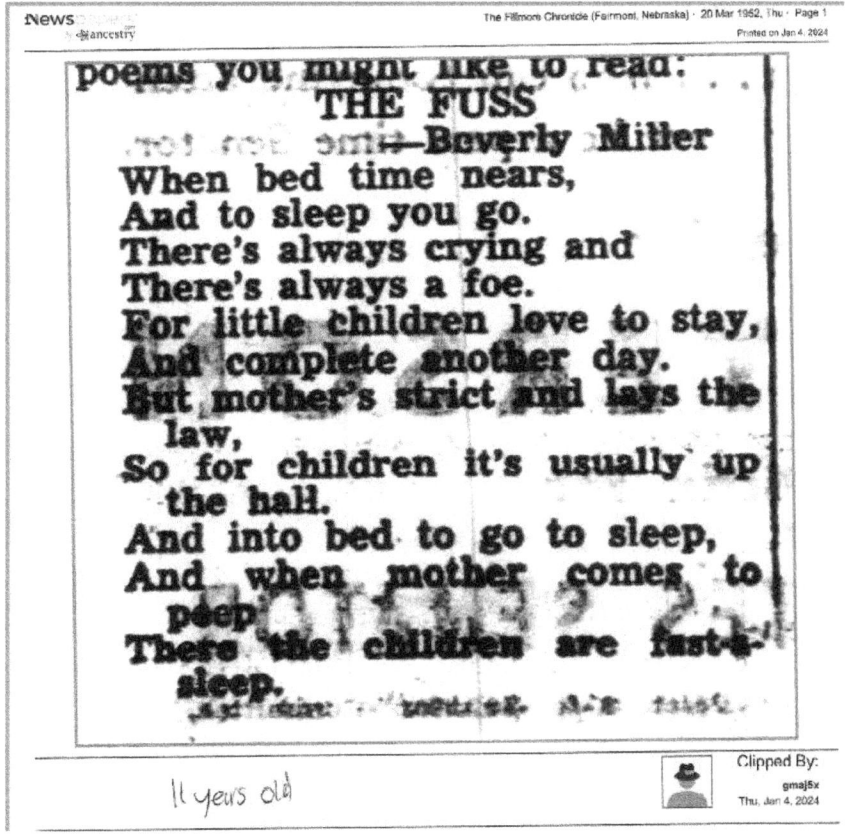

poems you might like to read:

THE FUSS

—Beverly Miller

When bed time nears,
And to sleep you go.
There's always crying and
There's always a foe.
For little children love to stay,
And complete another day.
But mother's strict and lays the
law,
So for children it's usually up
the hall.
And into bed to go to sleep,
And when mother comes to
peep
There the children are fast-a-
sleep.

11 years old

"The Fuss" — a poem written by eleven-year-old Beverly Miller, published in The Fillmore Chronicle in 1952. Even then, her words reflected an inner world far beyond her years.

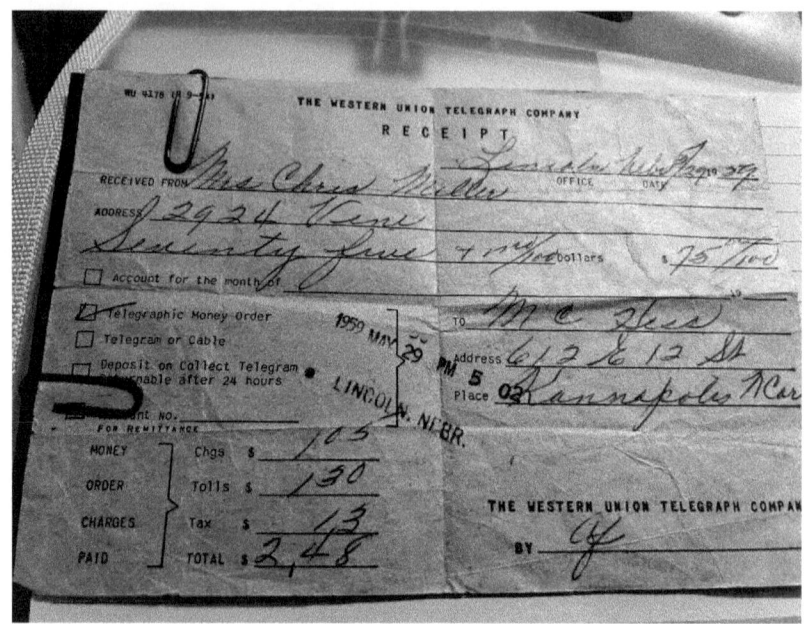

Western Union telegram sent in 1959 by Chris and Genevieve Miller to Beverly and her husband, Melvin. It offered $75 "for travel home," under the false pretense that Genevieve was gravely ill — a manipulation that drew Beverly back into Genevieve's control.

Teenaged Beverly in Nebraska, shortly before meeting Melvin Hess, with her brother Ted. The image reflects her transition from childhood hope to early adulthood overshadowed by control and hardship.

*Beverly with Genevieve and Christian Miller, and her brother Ted,
taken on Beverly's sixteenth birthday as of 04/02/1956.*

Marriage & Early Motherhood

Beverly and Melvin Hess on their wedding day, August 17, 1957. They were seventeen and eighteen — young, in love, and unaware that their future would soon be rewritten by forces beyond their control.

Beverly and Melvin dining with Genevieve and Christian Miller in 1958. Smiles mask the tension — the night Genevieve reportedly told Melvin, "She's your problem now."

www.ingramcontent.com/pod-product-compliance
Lightning Source LLC
Chambersburg PA
CBHW051147120626
46547CB00012B/982